Accounting in a Nutshell – Finance for the Non-specialist

Janet Walker

The Chartered Institute of Management Accountants
26 Chapter Street
London
SW1P 4NP

Accounting in a Nutshell – Finance for the Non-specialist

Copyright © Janet Walker 2001

First published in 2001 by:
The Chartered Institute of Management Accountants
26 Chapter Street
London
SW1P 4NP

ISBN 1 85971 495 1

The right of Janet Walker to be identified as author of this work has been asserted by her in accordance with sections 77 and 78 of the Copyright Designs and Patents Act 1988

The publishers of this book consider that it is a worthwhile contribution to discussion, without necessarily sharing the views expressed, which are those of the author.

No responsibility for loss occasioned to any person acting or refraining from action as a result of any material in this publication can be accepted by the author or publisher.

Contents

Part 1 Introduction

Part 2 Accounting statements

1

Who needs accounting statements? 9

4 Cash-flow reporting

5 The accounts of not-for-profit organisations

6 Interpreting financial statements: Part 1

Part 3 Using financial information to manage a business

8

9

Part 1 Introduction

About this text

This is a basic text for non-specialists who need an appreciation of the purposes and use of accounting information. It covers the basic principles of financial and management accounting for those who do not require detailed theoretical or technical knowledge. The text will provide a grounding and outline understanding to enable the reader to contribute in the workplace or to progress to further financial studies. It has been written assuming no prior financial knowledge, and without the use of accounting jargon.

Who should use this text?

This text is designed primarily for the following groups of people:

- Middle and junior managers who deal with financial information without really understanding the content
- Students who are studying accounting as a non-specialist subject, for example on a business studies or engineering course. The text will serve as a basic reference book to be used throughout the course. It will also be particularly helpful in providing the basic grounding which is required before moving on to the more technical and in-depth study of the subject that may be required on some courses
- Students who are embarking on a course of study to become a professional accountant. The basic understanding developed in this book will serve as a valuable base on which to build future professional studies.

The content of the text

The text is suitable for those interested in the accounts of profit-making organisations or not-for-profit organisations. It also gives equal weight to manufacturing and service organisations.

The text is divided into three parts.
Part 1 explains the scope of the text, who it is for, and how to use it effectively.
Part 2 begins with a review of the types of people who might use accounting statements and the sort of information that they might need.

It then introduces and reviews the main financial accounting statements: the profit and loss account (or income and expenditure account in not-for-profit organisations), the balance sheet and the cash flow statement. The final chapters of this section explain the basic techniques used to interpret the information contained within these financial statements.

Part 3 covers management accounting and the use of financial information to manage a business. It reviews the analysis and build-up of cost before going on to demonstrate the use of costs in management decision-making. This section concludes with a discussion of the use of budgetary planning and control.

The final section of the text contains a glossary of the major financial and management accounting terms used in the book, extracted from the Official Terminology of the Chartered Institute of Management Accountants.

How to use this text

The chapters are designed to be read in consecutive order. Knowledge and understanding are built in a cumulative fashion and the material contained in each chapter builds on the material in preceding chapters.

If your attention is focused on the accounts of not-for-profit organisations you are advised to read the earlier chapters based on the accounts of profit-making organisations. This is because the same principles apply in both sets of financial statements even though the organisations' ultimate objectives may differ. Similarly, if you are interested primarily in the financial statements of profit-making organisations you would benefit from working the exercises in Chapter 5, The accounts of not-for-profit organisations.

At convenient points throughout each chapter there are short exercises. You should take the time to try these exercises and think about the solutions. They will help you to test whether you have grasped the basic principles to that stage before proceeding with the subject matter.

At the end of most chapters you will find a series of review questions and self-test questions. The review questions will test your knowledge of the content of the chapter, referring you back to the relevant section of the chapter if you are unable to answer the question. The self-test questions are followed by outline answers, so that you can check your ability to apply your knowledge to a practical situation.

Thorough and diligent use of the self-testing mechanisms will be particularly useful for those readers who are not using the book as a part of a formal course of study.

Key to symbols

 Exercise

 Attention

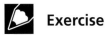 Solution

 Questions

 Review questions

Part 2 Accounting Statements

Who needs accounting statements?

1.1 Introduction

In the first part of this chapter we will be reviewing the groups of people who might use financial statements and thinking about what sort of information they might need. We will also be looking at the regulatory framework within which published financial statements are prepared.

We will then obtain an overview of the three main published financial statements (the profit and loss account or income and expenditure account, the balance sheet, and the cash-flow statement): what they are and what general purpose they serve.

1.2 Who uses financial statements and what sort of information might they need?

The list of people who might need the information provided by financial statements seems to grow longer every day. Some of these people are directly connected with the organisation, for example its employees and managers, others are not directly connected but they may be affected by its management of finance or its financial stability, for example the general public.

In this part of the chapter we will look at the user groups listed in Figure 1.1. This list is by no means exhaustive but it covers the main categories.

Figure 1.1: The users of financial information

- The owners of the business
- Managers, employees and prospective employees
- Lenders and potential lenders
- Customers
- Suppliers
- The government
- Donors/sponsors
- The public
- Analysts and advisers

Exercise

Look at each category of the users of accounts. Think about whether you belong in that particular user group. You will probably be surprised to realise that you fit into more than just one single category.

1.2.1 The owners of the business

In many small businesses the owner or owners are likely to be those responsible for the day-to-day running of the business. These owners need information to let them know whether they are making enough profits, whether they have sufficient cash to pay their bills as they fall due, to whom they owe money, who owes money to them, and so on.

As businesses begin to expand they may raise the money that they need for expansion from people who are not involved in the day-to-day running of the business. One way of doing this is to sell shares in the business and become a limited company. Shareholders are part-owners of the business. Among other things they will be concerned about the profitability of the company and how any profit is to be shared out or distributed to the shareholders. Furthermore, they will be concerned about the prospects for future returns on their investment. Potential future shareholders will also be interested in this sort of information when they are considering whether or not to purchase shares in the company.

Existing and future potential shareholders would also be interested in certain non-financial aspects of the company such as the activities it engages in and its policies so that they can decide if this is the sort of company with which they wish to be associated.

1.2.2 Managers, employees and prospective employees

The managers of a business need financial information to help them to manage the business. They need past financial information to help them monitor the progress of the business or their part of it, current information to carry out day-to-day operational management and control, and forecast financial information to plan activities in the future.

Employees and trades unions may consult the financial statements when they are negotiating their pay and terms of employment. Current and prospective employees might be wise to use the accounts as a basis for assessing the likelihood that the company will grow and prosper, or will it (and their job!) not exist this time next year?!

Exercise

Can you think of a reason why past employees might be interested in an organisation's accounts?

Solution

Will the organisation be able to meet its obligations to pay their pensions? (You may have thought of other, equally valid, reasons for past employees looking at the accounts.)

1.2.3 Lenders and potential lenders

Bankers and others who lend money to an organisation will need information concerning the organisation's ability to make interest payments in the short term and ultimately to repay the loan on its due date. They will also be concerned about the security for their loan, i.e. does the organisation have valuable items, or assets, that could be sold to raise the money to repay the loan if necessary?

Many user groups need short-term historical information (how has the business done and where is it now?) as well as longer-term future information (how well is the business likely to do in the future?).

1.2.4 Customers

Existing and potential customers will be concerned about whether the organisation will be able to provide the goods or services concerned. Some customer relationships can be relatively long term, in which case the supplier's financial stability can be very important. For example, a potential customer of a building firm would not want the builders to go into liquidation halfway through a construction job. Or an organisation might wish to ensure that the supplier of its computer support helpline will not suddenly go out of business.

1.2.5 Suppliers

Potential suppliers will need to ensure that their customer will be capable of paying for the goods and services supplied. Furthermore, as we saw above, many customer/supplier relationships are long term and involve a considerable investment of time and money to build up the necessary close relationship. A supplier (or customer) would wish to ensure the long-term viability of the other party before embarking on the work involved.

1.2.6 The government

For example, the taxation authorities will need to consult a company's financial statements and accounts to determine whether there is any taxation liability. Another example of a government body requiring financial information from organisations is the Charity Commission, which requires registered charities to submit annual returns. Other government departments and agencies may require financial and non-financial statistics to monitor the state of the economy.

1.2.7 Donors/sponsors

This category applies particularly to charities. Those people and organisations who donate money to charities, or who otherwise sponsor their activities, might use the financial statements to monitor whether they are happy with the way that the organisation is handling the funds available to it.

1.2.8 The public

This category includes taxpayers and ratepayers. The latter might particularly be interested in studying the local authority's financial statements to see whether they consider their rates are being spent wisely. Pressure groups and other special interest groups might be interested in studying a wide range of companies' accounts.

1.2.9 Analysts and advisers

These are the people who are advising investors, lenders and the general public. They will be advising all the sorts of people already considered in this list and so their information needs are likely to be similar. However, they are probably more technically competent to interpret and understand the financial statements.

Exercise

You are already aware that this is not an exhaustive list of the users of accounts. Can you think of three other users that have not been mentioned so far in this chapter?

Solution

You may have thought of some of the following users.

- Customs and Excise
- Accountants/auditors
- Fund managers
- Club members

- School parents
- Trustees
- Solicitors
- Information providers

- School governors
- The courts
- Credit-rating agencies
- Competitors

1.3 Published accounts and financial statements for internal use

1.3.1 Financial accounts and management accounts

Given the wide range of users that we have discussed and the diversity of their information needs, it should not surprise you to discover that there is a wealth of information available in an organisation's financial statements.

In the first part of this book we will be looking at the accounting information that is usually made available to the public – the published accounts or financial accounts. These include the profit and loss account, the balance sheet and the cash-flow statement.

In the second part we will look at the additional information that is necessary to help managers to run the business: the internal management accounts which are not usually made available to the public.

We will also be looking at the equivalent of the profit and loss account for not-for-profit organisations: the income and expenditure account.

1.3.2 The regulation of financial reporting

The many users of published financial information need to be confident that it provides a true and fair view of the particular organisation's financial affairs. For this reason a system of regulation has evolved to guide and control the content and presentation of published financial information.

Some of the regulations are statutory and are contained in the Companies Acts. Other non-statutory guidelines are provided in a series of accounting standards which are issued by the Accounting Standards Board (ASB). The standards are called Financial Reporting Standards (FRSs) and Statements of Standard Accounting Practice (SSAPs). They contain guidelines on matters ranging from the valuation of assets and accounting for leases to the format of cash-flow statements and accounting for VAT.

The regulatory system is continually evolving as the business environment changes: new FRSs are published as they are needed and existing SSAPs and FRSs are occasionally revised.

 The ASB is composed mainly of professional accountants who are appointed for their technical accounting skills. Before issuing an FRS the ASB will circulate draft proposals in a Financial Reporting Exposure Draft (FRED). Comments from the public are then taken into account before the final FRS is issued.

1.4 Three general questions

Most organisations publish three financial statements, usually annually but sometimes more frequently. These are the profit and loss account, the balance sheet and the cash-flow statement. In general terms these help to provide the answers to three basic questions about an organisation.

No matter which user group we are considering, it is possible to express in very general terms the questions that most users will be asking when they are reviewing an organisation's published statements. Basically someone who is reading accounts will be trying to find the answer to one or more of the following three questions.

Question 1: What *return* is this organisation making?

For example, the owners and potential investors will be interested in what sort of return they can earn from their investment in the business. The Inland Revenue will wish to calculate the amount of any taxation due. Competitors will be interested in whether the business is earning a higher or lower return than they are achieving themselves. These people will need to know:

- What revenue is the organisation generating?
- What costs are they incurring in generating that revenue, and do the costs exceed the revenue?
- If the organisation is making a profit, what have they decided to do with it? How much has been reinvested in the business for future growth? How much has been taken out of the business by the owners?

Questions of this sort can be answered by looking at the profit and loss account, which will be the subject of the next chapter.

Exercise

In a not-for-profit organisation it is obviously not appropriate to ask 'what return is the organisation making?' Can you think of the sort of questions that might be asked in place of this one?

Solution

- What revenue is the organisation generating?
- What costs are they incurring in generating that revenue, and do the costs exceed the revenue?
- If the organisation is generating a surplus, what have they decided to do with the surplus?

Notice the similarity between these questions and those asked about a profit-making organisation. The main difference is the use of the word 'surplus' instead of 'profit'.

In a not-for-profit organisation these questions can be answered by looking at the income and expenditure account, which is the equivalent of a profit and loss account for these organisations.

We will be studying income and expenditure accounts in Chapter 5.

Question 2: What is the *risk* associated with this organisation?

For example, a potential lender will wish to know whether there is a risk that the money to be lent will not be repaid. A supplier who has been asked to send goods with payment due later will want to know whether the bill will be paid when it falls due. These people will need to know:

- What does the organisation owe to other people?
- What valuable items (assets) does the organisation possess as security for my loan?
- How much of the business's capital is borrowed and how much has been invested by the owners?

The term used to describe the relative proportion of borrowed money and the owner's investment is 'gearing'. You will be learning about this in Chapter 7.

One of the first places to look in order to answer questions such as these is the organisation's balance sheet. We will be considering the balance sheet in detail in Chapter 3.

Question 3: Does the organisation have sufficient *cash*?

Later in this book we will see that it is not uncommon for an organisation to be generating a profit or surplus and yet still be desperately short of cash. We will be seeing the reasons for this, which include the need to spend money in advance of making sales or carrying out fund-raising activities. The ability of the organisation to generate cash from its activities and to use the cash wisely is of utmost importance to its survival.

The questions which users will be asking in respect of cash include:

- How much cash does the organisation generate from its activities?
- Is there sufficient cash to cover the organisation's investment for future growth?
- If there is not sufficient cash from the organisation's own activities, what sources are used to make up the cash shortfall?

The cash-flow statement will help to provide the answers to these questions. We will be looking at cash-flow statements in Chapter 4.

A mnemonic that you might find useful to remember 'the three questions' is 'the three Rs':

- *Return? – profit and loss/income and expenditure account*
- *Risk? – balance sheet*
- *Readies? – cash-flow statement.*

1.5 Summary

1. There are many different groups of people who might need to read and understand an organisation's financial statements.
2. The content and presentation of published financial statements is regulated partly by the Companies Acts and partly by a series of accounting standards.
3. The three main statements published by most organisations for users external to the business are the profit and loss account, the balance sheet and the cash-flow statement.

Review questions
1. Why might an organisation's customers and suppliers need to read its financial statements? (sections 1.2.4, 1.2.5)
2. What is meant by the acronym FRS? (section 1.3.2)
3. What are the three general questions that can be answered by looking at an organisation's financial statements? (section 1.4)

2 The profit and loss account

2.1 Introduction

In this chapter we will be looking at the profit and loss account: what it is and what is its purpose. Even if your attention is focused on the accounts of not-for-profit organisations you should read this chapter because the principles that will be discussed apply in the preparation of the income and expenditure account. Throughout the chapter we will be using the following typical example as a basis for our discussion.

Example plc: profit and loss account for the year ended 31 December, year 7

	£000
Turnover	5,590
Cost of sales	4,100
Gross profit	1,490
Other expenses	840
Profit before interest and taxation	650
Interest payable	50
Profit before taxation	600
Taxation	135
Net profit for the year	465
Dividends	230
Retained profit for the year	235

2.2 The title of the statement

2.2.1 Public limited company

The statement above is the profit and loss account for Example **plc**. The acronym 'plc' stands for 'public limited company'. A limited company is one which has sold shares to investors as a way of raising the capital to fund its growth. If you buy a share in a company then you literally do buy for yourself a share in that company's fortunes. If, say, a company sells in total one million shares and you buy one share, then you own a millionth share in the company. A millionth of all the valuable items that it possesses, its assets, belong to you and a millionth of all of its profits belong to you. Luckily you will not have to shoulder a millionth of its losses because of the concept of limited liability.

Limited liability means that the people who have purchased shares in the company (the shareholders) have limited their liability to the amount they have paid for their share. If the company goes into liquidation all they will lose will be the amount they have paid or agreed to pay for their share. Hence the term 'limited' in 'public limited company'.

The term 'public' means that our company, Example, is free to offer its shares for sale to the public if it wishes. This contrasts with a private company which may not offer its shares to the public. If our company was a private company then its title would be Example Limited.

Exercise

Have a look at the titles of some of the companies that you come across during the next few days. Are they public limited companies (e.g. ABC plc), private limited companies (e.g. XYZ Limited) or are they not limited companies at all (e.g. Bill Jones and Company – without the word 'Limited')?

2.2.2 Profit and loss account for the year

The profit and loss account is a financial statement which shows the profit or loss earned by the business in a particular accounting period. In our case the accounting period is one year but profit and loss accounts are sometimes published for shorter periods of, say, six months.

An important point to grasp is that the title clearly states that the account is for year 7. This means that every item shown in this account belongs as a cost or revenue in year 7. The account will not show items that have been paid in advance for year 8, neither will it show items for year 6 that were paid late, during year 7.

Later in this chapter we will see how these items - known as prepayments and accruals – are dealt with in the profit and loss account and we will work through a numerical example.

This is the application of the **accruals concept**, which is the principle that costs and revenues are recognised as they are earned or incurred and are matched with one another in the profit and loss account of the period to which they relate, irrespective of when the cash is actually received or paid out.

2.3 Calculating the gross profit

2.3.1 Turnover

The first item shown on the profit and loss account is the turnover. This is the amount to be received from customers in return for the provision of Example's goods or services. As soon as a sale is made it is shown in the profit and loss account, even if the money has not yet been received from the customer. Other terms used instead of turnover include sales revenue or sales income.

You may be starting to appreciate how a company can be showing a profit in its profit and loss account but still have no cash.

2.3.2 Cost of sales

The cost of sales is deducted from turnover. This cost is the cost of the goods or services that have been sold to generate the turnover for the period.

An alternative term used to describe cost of sales is 'cost of goods sold'.

The cost of goods sold is most easily derived for a manufacturing company. For example, in a company which manufactures washing machines it is the actual cost of producing the machines for sale: the materials used, the wages paid to manufacturing labour, the overhead cost of running the factory, etc.

Another term which may be used to describe this type of cost is 'direct cost'. We will return to consider direct costs in a later chapter.

The cost of goods sold would not include 'support costs' such as advertising and head office secretarial costs. These would be treated as 'other expenses' later in the profit and loss account.

It is also fairly easy to derive the cost of sales or cost of goods sold for a retailing organisation such as a supermarket. In this case it would probably be the amount paid to the supplier for the goods to be sold to the supermarket's customers.

It is not so easy to derive the cost of sales for a service organisation. For example, for a haulage company it would be the actual costs of providing the haulage service to the customer, including fuel costs and drivers' wages. It would not include support costs such as those mentioned earlier.

Exercise

Have a think about the company you work for or a company with which you are familiar. Which costs would you say they should include as a part of cost of sales and which costs should be treated as 'other expenses'? You can probably appreciate that the decision as to whether to treat a particular cost as a part of cost of sales or as an 'other expense' calls for some subjective judgement.

2.3.3 Gross profit

This is the first measure of a company's profit which is calculated by deducting the cost of sales from the turnover. It shows whether the company sold its goods and services for more than they cost to provide. You can see that if a company does not make a gross profit then it is really in trouble! It is the gross profit that is used to pay all the other expenses of running the business.

Another term used to describe gross profit is 'gross margin'.

2.4   Calculating the net profit for the year

2.4.1 Other expenses

These include all the costs, apart from interest, which have not been included as a part of cost of sales. The main groups of cost in this category are distribution, selling and administration costs.

However, it is not simply a case of picking up the expenditure balances from the accounts and showing them as the costs for the year. We have seen that the cost shown in the profit and loss account must be only the cost that relates to the year. Therefore we have to adjust for any items paid in advance (prepayments) or for any bills that are still unpaid or owing (accruals).

For instance, if Example has paid its insurance bill for the period up to the end of March year 8 then it would not be fair to charge all of that insurance cost as a cost of running the business in year 7. This would overstate the cost for year 7 and understate the cost for year 8. The amount of the insurance that relates to January, February and March year 8 is deducted from the insurance balance and only the remainder is shown as the insurance cost for year 7.

Furthermore, Example may have paid its latest head office telephone bill on 30 November year 7. To be able to include a fair telephone cost for the period it will be necessary to estimate the telephone cost for December and add this on to the amount paid so far. Can you imagine how difficult it is to produce an accurate estimate? It is hard enough to estimate what your own telephone bill will be for the next quarter, but when you are estimating for dozens or even hundreds of telephones and data processing lines the task is extremely difficult.

In the next chapter we will see what happens to the part of the insurance bill that has been deducted (the prepayment) and to the extra that has been added to the telephone bill (the accrual).

For other types of accrual such as a newspaper advertisement that is still to be invoiced, the accountant often needs to rely on the relevant manager informing the accounts department when invoices are still expected. Those readers who are or who work for budget managers might now appreciate why the accounts department asks them for their accruals at the end of each period.

The amount of £840 shown in Example plc's profit and loss account is therefore not simply the total of the balances shown on the company's accounting records. The amounts paid during the year will have been adjusted (albeit often subjectively) to arrive at the best possible estimate of a true and fair cost for the year.

Another subjective item included within 'other costs' is depreciation. We shall see what this is and how it is calculated in the next chapter.

Attempt the following exercise to adjust for accruals and prepayments. Do not worry if you get it wrong or if you are not quite sure how to begin. The main thing is to ensure that you understand the solution and the reason for the adjustments before reading on.

Exercise

A company rents its office photocopier. The basic rental payments are made in advance and in addition at the end of each quarter the company pays 2 pence per copy made during the last quarter. The latest invoice for photocopier expenses was paid on 31 March. Relevant information is as follows.

- Latest rental payment made on 31 March: £90 for the quarter ended 30 June
- Number of photocopies taken, 1–30 April = 9,800
- Photocopier charges account balance as at 30 April = £2,700

What is the correct cost for photocopier charges to be included in the company's profit and loss account for the period ended 30 April?

Solution

	£
Account balance	2,700
Less rental paid in advance for May and June ($\frac{2}{3} \times$ £90)	(60)
	2,640
Plus amount owing for copy charges for April (9,800 × £0.02)	196
Amount to be shown in the profit and loss account	2,836

2.4.2 Profit before interest and taxation

Another term used to describe this profit measure is **operating profit**. It is calculated by deducting the other expenses from the gross profit. Later in this book we will see that this is a very important profit measure because it is the profit over which operational managers can exercise day-to-day control. It is the profit measure which they can most easily influence because it is not affected by factors such as taxation and interest which are largely outside their control.

2.4.3 Interest payable

This is the amount of interest for the year which Example plc must pay on all its loans, borrowings and overdrafts, etc. This is deducted to arrive at the profit before taxation.

2.4.4 Taxation

Companies pay corporation tax on their profits. It is outside the scope of this book to examine the taxation charge in any detail but basically companies pay taxation at a very similar percentage rate to that paid by individuals. However, there are many adjustments which must be made to the profit figure in order to calculate the company's taxable profit. These adjustments will be discussed with the Inland Revenue before the final corporation tax charge is agreed.

2.5 Dividends and retained profits

2.5.1 The profit attributable to the shareholders

Once the taxation charge has been deducted the remainder of the profit belongs to the shareholders: the accounting jargon for this is 'the profit attributable to the shareholders'. All other costs and charges have been paid and the company directors can now distribute or pay out this profit to the shareholders in the form of cash dividends if they wish.

In practice, the directors are unlikely to pay out all the profits in the form of dividends. One reason is that the shareholders may have to pay income tax on the dividends and they may not be too keen on this! However, the main reason for not paying out all the profits is that the profits provide a ready source of finance to help the company to grow. If the company wants to take on more customers and provide more products or services it will need capital to do this. One of the best places to obtain this extra capital is to use the profits that the business is generating.

If the value of the company grows as it expands then it follows that the value of a share in the company will also grow. The shareholders will therefore make a capital gain and so will probably be quite happy not to have received cash dividends from the company.

Retained profit is therefore an important source of finance for a company. This profit is taken to reserves, which will be discussed in more detail in the next chapter when we look at the contents of the balance sheet.

If a company has made a loss it may still be able to pay dividends out of the retained profits from previous years. The accounting jargon for this is 'paying a dividend out of reserves'.

Exercise
Look again at the profit and loss account for Example plc. What would you say is the answer to the question 'what profit did Example plc make in year 7?'

Solution
This is really a bit of a trick question. Any of the following answers would be correct.

- Gross profit = £1,490,000
- Operating profit = £650,000
- Profit before taxation = £600,000
- Net profit = £465,000

You could even add taxable profit to the list, if we had the figure available. The taxable profit figure is not shown on a company's profit and loss account. It is derived after various adjustments have been made to the net profit for the year, usually in consultation with the Inland Revenue.

The problem with the question set in the last exercise was that it was imprecise. You should never refer to profit without specifying to which particular profit measure you are referring.

2.6 FRS 3 *Reporting financial performance*

Some profit and loss accounts might not be as straightforward as the one which we have analysed for Example plc. One complication arises from the reporting requirements of FRS 3 *Reporting Financial Performance*. This standard requires companies' profit and loss accounts to analyse turnover and operating profit between the following.

- Continuing operations
- Acquisitions
- Discontinued operations

This means that if a company has discontinued a part of its business, the accounts must show separately the operating profit and turnover earned from that part of the business during the year, up to the point when it was sold or when it ceased activity. The accounts must also show separately the operating profit and turnover earned from any new businesses acquired during the year (acquisitions). The figures shown must relate only to the performance since the acquisition took place. The remainder of the business will be the continuing operations, i.e. the part of the business which is not affected by any discontinuance or acquisitions, which must also be analysed separately.

For instance, if Example plc had discontinued part of its business during the year its profit and loss account might look like the account shown opposite.

Example plc: profit and loss account for the year ended 31 December, year 7

	£000
Turnover	
Continuing operations	5,290
Discontinued operations	300
	5,590
Cost of sales	4,100
Gross profit	1,490
Other expenses	840
Operating profit	650
analysed between:	
Continuing operations	630
Discontinued operations	20
Interest payable	50
Profit before taxation	600
Taxation	135
Net profit for the year	465
Dividends	230
Retained profit for the year	235

You can see that the total figures have not altered, but there is more information about how much of the turnover and operating profit has come from continuing operations. These figures are likely to be more useful to the users of the accounts if, perhaps, they are trying to assess the future prospects of Example plc.

2.7 Summary

1. The profit and loss account is a financial statement which shows the profit or loss earned by the organisation in a particular accounting period.
2. Every item in a period's profit and loss account is a cost or revenue that relates specifically to that period, irrespective of when the cash is actually received or paid out. Many of the items are estimated amounts which involve subjective judgements.
3. There are several different profit measures which can be used to monitor the performance of a business.
4. Not all the profits attributable to shareholders are paid out as dividends. It is usual for some profits to be retained in reserves to finance the company's plans for growth.

5. FRS3 requires companies' profit and loss accounts to analyse turnover and operating profit between continuing operations, acquisitions and discontinued operations.

We will look at the interpretation of profit and loss accounts in a later chapter

Review questions

1. What is meant by 'limited liability'? (section 2.2.1)
2. What is the main practical difference between a public limited company and a private limited company? (section 2.2.1)
3. What is the accruals concept? (section 2.2.2)
4. What is cost of sales? (section 2.3.2)
5. How is gross profit calculated? (section 2.3.3)
6. What is operating profit? (section 2.4.2)

Self-test questions

1. JS Ltd has just completed its first year of trading, the year ending 30 September Year 3.

Information concerning advertising costs and rent is as follows.

Advertising
Adverts were placed in a trade journal published on 1 March and 1 September. One month's credit is available on all invoices.

Advert placed	Cost	Invoice date	Invoice paid
1 March Year 3	£2,890	6 March Yr 3	4 April Yr 3
1 Sept Year 3	£3,220	5 Sept Yr 3	(not yet paid)

Rent
Rent = £18,000 per annum, payable quarterly in advance.

Payments made during the first year:		
4 October	Year 2	£4,500
28 December	Year 2	£4,500
29 March	Year 3	£4,500
29 June	Year 3	£4,500
28 September	Year 3	£4,500

Required

What is the correct charge in the profit and loss account for the year ending 30 September Year 3 in respect of:

(a) advertising;
(b) rent.

2. Extracts from RP plc's latest published profit and loss account are as follows.

	Year 12 £m	Year 11 £m	Change %
Turnover			
Continuing operations	547	480	
Acquisition	60	–	
Total	607	480	+26
Operating profit			
Continuing operations	84	82	
Acquisition	15	–	
Total	99	82	+21

Required

Comment on RP plc's turnover and profit performance in year 12 compared with year 11, and discuss the suitability of this information as a basis for forecasting the results for year 13.

Answers to self-test questions

1.

(a) *Advertising*

The advert placed on 1 September represents a valid cost to be included in the profit and loss account for the year ending 30 September year 3, even though the invoice has not yet been paid. The correct charge in the profit and loss account for the year is:

£2,890 paid + £3,220 accrued = £6,110

(b) *Rent*

The correct charge for the year is the annual rent figure of £18,000. The profit and loss account will be charged with £18,000 and the extra £4,500 paid in advance is a prepayment.

2. *Turnover*

Total turnover has increased by 26 per cent but a large proportion of this increase has come from an acquisition.

The continuing operations which have been in existence all year have generated a 14 per cent increase in turnover.

If we wished to use these figures as a basis for forecasting the turnover for year 13 we would need to know the date of the acquisition. The £60m turnover shown for the acquisition is the turnover generated since the date of acquisition.

Operating profit

Operating profit has increased by 21 per cent but again a large proportion of this increase has come from an acquisition.

The continuing operations generated only little more than a 2 per cent increase in operating profit, despite the 14 per cent increase in turnover. Costs must have increased at a faster rate than turnover.

Virtually all of the increase in operating profit was achieved through acquisition, therefore the 21 per cent total annual growth in profit cannot be expected to be maintained in future.

If we wished to use these figures as a basis for forecasting the operating profit for year 13 we would need to know the date of the acquisition. The £15m operating profit shown for the acquisition is the operating profit generated since the date of acquisition.

The balance sheet

3.1 Introduction

In this chapter we will be looking at the balance sheet: what it is and what is its purpose; what it does and does not show. We will be using a profit-making public limited company as the basis for our discussion. However, the same basic principles apply to the preparation of balance sheets for all types of organisation, ranging from the smallest not-for-profit tennis club to the largest public limited company. Throughout this chapter we will be using the following illustration of a typical company's balance sheet:

Example plc: balance sheet as at 31 December year 7

	£000	£000
Fixed assets		
Intangible assets		250
Tangible assets		2,400
Investments		35
		2,685
Current assets		
Stock	328	
Debtors	533	
Cash at bank and in hand	120	
	981	
Current liabilities		
Creditors: amounts falling due within one year	600	
Working capital		381
Total assets less current liabilities		3,066
Capital and reserves		
Called-up share capital		2,200
Reserves – retained profits		580
Shareholders' funds		2,780
Creditors falling due after more than one year		286
Capital employed		3,066

3.2 What is a balance sheet?

3.2.1 The balance sheet must balance

A balance sheet is a statement which shows the things of value that an organisation owns (the assets), as well as the sources of finance used to buy them. The statement is divided into two parts. The top part usually gives details of the assets and the bottom part lists the sources of finance. Logically the total of the two parts must be equal, i.e. the total value of the assets must be equal to the total amount of finance raised to buy them. In other words, the balance sheet must balance. If you look at the bottom of the balance sheet for Example plc you will see that the total capital invested in the business (the capital employed) is £3,066,000. This is the total of one half of the balance sheet. The top half shows where this money is invested and in this chapter we will be looking separately at each of these items.

Balance sheets are occasionally presented the 'other way up', i.e. capital is listed in the top part and the assets in the bottom part. You may also see balance sheets presented 'side by side' with the capital on the left-hand side and the assets on the right.

3.2.2 The balance sheet date

Look carefully at the title of the balance sheet. Then turn back and look at the title of the profit and loss account at the beginning of Chapter 2. Can you see the difference? The title of the profit and loss account clearly indicates that it shows the results for the whole year, whereas the balance sheet states *as at* 31 December year 7. The balance sheet is like a photograph of the business taken on the last day of the financial year.

Many asset balances are constantly changing, and the balances shown on the balance sheet for some assets, for example stock and cash, may be nothing like the balances that were in the business at the end of, say, November. Furthermore they are highly likely to be different again by the end of January year 8. All the balances shown on the statement are simply the balances that existed on the last day of the financial year. This will be an important point to bear in mind when you come to learn about the interpretation of financial statements.

The values of some of the items on the balance sheet are more likely to change than others. You will appreciate which are likely to change once you have finished studying this chapter.

3.2.3 The use of columns in the balance sheet

People are often confused by the use of columns in the balance sheet. Before going on to the detail of the balance sheet, and to learn the meaning of each of the terms, look carefully at Example's balance sheet and check that you can see which figures have been added together to derive each total and subtotal.

The columns in the balance sheet are used to calculate any required subtotals. For example, a separate column is used to calculate the current asset total of £981,000 and then the current liabilities of £600,000 are deducted from this. The net balance of £381,000 is called the working capital and this final total is brought out into the end column to be added to the fixed asset total.

The columns have no particular meaning: they are simply providing space to do separate subtotal calculations, so that the right-hand column does not become too cluttered.

3.3 Capital expenditure and revenue expenditure

When money is put into a business there are basically two areas in which it can be invested. It can either be used to purchase items that are going to be kept in the business for several years or it can be invested in or used to pay for items that will be used relatively rapidly in the day-to-day running of the business.

Items which are going to be kept for several years and which are not bought with the intention of resale are called fixed assets. Examples are buildings, machinery, office equipment and vehicles. Money spent on fixed assets is called capital expenditure and it will benefit the business for several years.

Money spent on day-to-day running costs where the benefit will be rapidly used up is called revenue expenditure. Examples are salaries, telephone bills and the purchase of stock items for resale. It is easy to see that the first two items in this list (salaries and telephone bills) are items of a short-term nature and that the benefit from the expenditure will be rapidly used up. The purchase of stock is slightly different. The stock is an asset of the business (it has value) but because the intention is to use it relatively quickly for resale, it is classified as a current asset. You can see that Example plc has some stock included under current assets in the balance sheet. As a general rule, current assets are those which are going to be used up within a year.

Now that you have a general idea of the different types of expenditure in a business we will look in detail at each of the items on Example plc's balance sheet.

3.4 Fixed assets

3.4.1 Tangible and intangible fixed assets

We have already seen that fixed assets are those assets which are going to be kept and used in the business for several years. If you look at Example plc's balance sheet you will see that the first two types of fixed asset shown are intangible fixed assets and tangible fixed assets. Tangible fixed assets are those which have a physical identity, for example office equipment and delivery vehicles. Intangible fixed assets are those which do not have a physical identity, but which have some value to the business, for example patents and trademarks.

 Another intangible fixed asset that you might come across is goodwill. We will return to discuss goodwill later in the chapter.

3.4.2 Depreciation

You should recall that the profit and loss account for the year shows the fair cost of running the business for the year. Think about what happens when a fixed asset, for example a delivery van costing £22,000, is purchased. The £22,000 is paid out to the supplier, but it would not really be fair to charge the whole of that £22,000 in the profit and loss account. Otherwise the profit for that year would be relatively low and then in later years the business would be using the vehicle without suffering any charge in the profit and loss account for the year. Profits would be distorted and managers and others who are using the accounts would not find it easy to monitor the business's performance.

This problem is resolved by sharing out the original cost of the asset over the years that will benefit from its use. Suppose in our example of the delivery van we assumed that it would last the business for four years, after which time it would be sold for £2,000. This means that over the years we are using it we will have used up £20,000 of the van's value (£22,000 cost less £2,000 final sales value). A fair share of the loss of value for each year could therefore be £5,000.

$$\frac{£22,000 - £2,000}{4 \text{ years}} = £5,000 \text{ per year}$$

This £5,000 is known as the depreciation charge for the year.

This method of calculating depreciation is called straight-line depreciation. Other methods commonly used charge greater amounts in the earlier years and less in the later years of the asset's life.

The depreciation charge is applied as follows:

Year 1 In the first year of the van's life £5,000 depreciation will be charged to the profit and loss account as the fair cost of using the van for the year. The remaining £17,000 (£22,000 less £5,000) will be shown in the balance sheet at the end of year 1 under tangible fixed assets. This £17,000 is known as the **net book value** of the fixed asset.

Year 2 In the second year another £5,000 depreciation will be charged in that year's profit and loss account. The remaining £12,000 will be shown in the balance sheet at the end of year 2 under tangible fixed assets.

The value of the delivery van used up by the business will thus be shared out over the years that receive the benefit.

	Charge to profit and loss account	*Net book value shown in balance sheet at end of year*
	£	£
Year 1	5,000	17,000
Year 2	5,000	12,000
Year 3	5,000	7,000
Year 4	5,000	2,000
	20,000	

Notice that the final value shown in the balance sheet at the end of the van's useful life is £2,000, i.e. the amount we expect to sell it for.

Exercise

A landscape gardening company has purchased a new fleet of lawnmowers for £5,000. They expect to use the lawnmowers for three years, after which time they will be sold for a total of £500. Using straight-line depreciation (equal depreciation charges for each year) produce a table which shows, for each of the three years, the depreciation charge in the profit and loss account and the net book value to be shown in the balance sheet.

Solution

$$\text{Annual depreciation charge} = \frac{£5,000 - £500}{3} = £1,500 \text{ per annum}$$

	Depreciation charge to profit and loss account	Net book value shown in balance sheet at end of year
	£	£
Year 1	1,500	3,500
Year 2	1,500	2,000
Year 3	1,500	500
	4,500	

3.4.3 Cost sharing, not valuation

It is important for you to appreciate that the aim of the depreciation charge is simply to share out the cost of the asset over the years that it is used. In the example of the delivery van, the £17,000 shown in the balance sheet for year 1 is simply the amount of the delivery van's cost left in the accounts which has not yet been shared out or charged to profit and loss. It is not a valuation of the asset, therefore the term net book **value** can be rather misleading.

We could just as easily, and quite defensibly, have stated that the van would last for five years instead of four. The annual depreciation charge would then be £4,000 [$(£22,000 - £2,000)/_5$] and the net book value at the end of year 1 would be £18,000 (£22,000 less £4,000 depreciation). The same asset, in the same business, is apparently 'worth' £1,000 more – and the profit for the year is £1,000 more.

In this example the figures involved are relatively small, but imagine what a difference a change in depreciation policy could make in companies with very large fixed assets, for example aircraft and expensive manufacturing machinery. For this reason companies are required to state their depreciation policy in their published accounts. To give you an idea of what this statement might say, here is part of the statement from the Annual Report of Whitbread plc for 1999/2000. It is included on the page headed 'Accounting Policies'.

*'**Tangible fixed assets** ... Depreciable fixed assets are written off on a straight-line basis over their estimated useful lives, as follows: ... Vehicles are depreciated over four to ten years.'*

3.4.4 Amortisation

Amortisation is similar to depreciation but the term is usually used to describe the 'depreciation' of intangible fixed assets. For example, J Sainsbury plc's accounting policy statement for 2000 includes the following in the section headed 'Fixed assets'.

'Acquired pharmacy licenses are included in intangible assets and are stated at cost less amortisation. These are amortised on a straight-line basis over a useful economic life of fifteen years.'

You can see that the effect of the amortisation charge is the same as a depreciation charge. The cost of a pharmacy license is spread over the profit and loss accounts of the years that benefit from the acquisition of the license. At the end of each year the balance sheet will show the amount of the original cost that has not yet been 'shared out' to any of the profit and loss accounts, i.e. the licenses are 'stated at cost less amortisation'.

3.4.5 Revaluing fixed assets

Some fixed assets may increase in value, for example property values tend to increase over time. In this situation the company can revalue the property, based on the advice of a suitably qualified professional. Depreciation of the property must then be based on the new, higher revalued figure in the balance sheet, using the same principles that you learned about earlier. For this reason you might see the statement 'tangible fixed assets are shown at cost or valuation, less accumulated depreciation'.

You might think that it is strange to depreciate properties, but they do not last forever! Most types of property are revalued regularly and then depreciated over a long time period of, say, 50 years.

3.4.6 Investments

A company may decide to buy shares in another company and hold them on a long-term basis. These shares would be shown under fixed assets as investments. If you look at Example plc's balance sheet you will see that they are holding £35,000 of fixed asset investments. There are many reasons why one company might decide to buy shares in another, including the following:

- To gain some control over the supply of an important material or component
- To spread or reduce their business risk. To give a simplified example of this, a manufacturer of sun hats might purchase shares in a company which manufactures raincoats. Then, come rain or shine, the company should be able to earn a profit!

- To engage in a joint venture which is beneficial to both companies.

 Sometimes you might see investments listed under current assets. These are shares which the company has bought as a short-term investment and they are usually held for less than one year.

3.5 Working capital

3.5.1 The flow of money round the working capital cycle

The remainder of an organisation's money that is not invested in fixed assets will be invested in its working capital. Figure 3.1 shows how money flows around the working capital cycle.

Figure 3.1: The working capital cycle

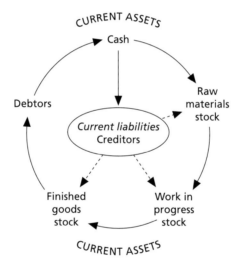

Imagine that you are starting a new business. Let's assume that the business is going to produce decorated plant pots to sell in garden centres. Once you have raised some money or capital, you might purchase the fixed assets that you need for your operations (for example, a kiln, delivery vehicles and so on). The remainder of the money will initially be held as a current asset in the form of cash.

 Remember that current assets are generally those that are going to be used up within a year.

Now the business will need to start using that cash to produce plant pots that can be sold at a profit. First you must buy some raw materials stock: clay, paint and so on. Some of the current asset of cash has now been converted into a different form of current asset: raw materials stock. Now you will need to start converting the raw materials into saleable plant pots. Cash will be spent on wages, power, telephone bills, etc. as the business carries on its operations and converts some of the materials into pots. A point will be reached where the material is no longer basic untouched raw material, but neither is it in a state to sell to the customer. This is known as work in progress stock, another form of current asset.

Finally, after more cash has been spent on day-to-day running costs (remember this is called revenue expenditure) the work in progress is converted into finished goods stock: another type of current asset.

You should be able to trace the movement of cash in the flower pot business round the working capital cycle in Figure 3.1.

Now it is time to deliver the pots to the garden centre to sell them. The cash from the sale can then be used to buy more raw materials, convert this into work in progress, and so on round the cycle again. Unfortunately it is not that simple!

Most businesses work on credit. The customer (in this case the garden centre) will usually expect to be given time to pay. This means that the current asset of finished goods, once sold, is converted into a different form of current asset: debtors. You can see this in Figure 3.1. Debtors are customers who are taking time to pay for the goods or services that they have received.

Another term often used instead of debtors is 'accounts receivable'.

Eventually the debtors should pay what is owed, and the cash can then be sent off again round the working capital cycle.

Contrast the circulating nature of the investment in working capital with the more permanent nature of the investment in fixed assets.

You should be able to appreciate that in some businesses it may take quite a long time for cash to move round the cycle described so far. Meanwhile cash is being continually pumped into the cycle every day. If no cash comes out 'the other end' then the business will very soon grind to a halt because it is starved of cash. Therefore it is vital to control the working capital cycle, to keep the cash moving round as quickly as possible, rather like the blood in a human body. If the blood stops pumping, the body will die!

A slight buffer is provided by creditors. A creditworthy business should be able to obtain credit for many of the items and services that it purchases. Creditors are people who are giving the business time to pay. Therefore it is possible, for example, to start some raw materials moving round the cycle before the cash has to be found to pay for them.

Another term often used instead of creditors is 'accounts payable'.

Eventually the business will have to find the cash to pay the creditors and it is vital that it is there when it is needed. In the next chapter we will see that cash-flow forecasting helps to ensure that cash is available when it is needed.

Exercise

Can you think of one type of business that would have a relatively short working capital cycle, i.e. where cash would not take long to travel round the cycle to be converted into cash once more? And can you think of a type of business that would have a relatively long working capital cycle?

Solution

A retailing organisation such as a supermarket chain would have a relatively short working capital cycle. Stocks are not held for long, and debtors may be non-existent because customers pay for their goods in cash.

A heavy manufacturing organisation such as a shipbuilder would have a relatively long working capital cycle. It takes a long time to convert the raw materials into finished goods, and so on.

3.5.2 Valuing the working capital

The balance sheet shows the amount of money invested in the organisation's working capital on the date that the balance sheet was prepared. Looking at Example plc's balance sheet you will see that the total value of the working capital is £381,000.

Extract from Example plc's balance sheet as at 31 December year 7

	£000	£000
Current assets		
Stock	328	
Debtors	533	
Cash at bank and in hand	120	
	981	
Current liabilities		
Creditors: amounts falling due within one year	600	
Working capital		381

The current assets are listed together and a subtotal is given for their value (£981,000). From this is deducted the value of the current liabilities (the creditors: £600,000) to arrive at the total value for working capital.

Just to remind you what the second column in the balance sheet is for! This is simply a 'working column' so that the value of the working capital can be calculated without cluttering the end column. The 'answer' to the calculation, i.e. the value of the working capital, (£981,000 – £600,000 = £381,000) is brought out into the end column.

Many balance sheets do not use the term working capital to describe this balance (£381,000). Instead they use the term **net current assets**. What does this mean?

In accounting, 'net' means 'after something has been deducted'. Hence a salary slip might show first the gross salary, then the deductions for tax, pension, etc., to arrive at the **net** salary. You have already seen that a profit and loss account shows first the gross profit, then the overheads are deducted to arrive at the **net** profit. Therefore, if you see the word 'net' in an accounting statement you simply have to look further up the statement to see what has been deducted. In this case the current liabilities (creditors) have been deducted from the current assets to deduce the net value remaining, i.e. the net current assets.

In some organisations the current liabilities exceed the current assets. In this situation they would show 'net current liabilities' instead of 'net current assets'. This does not necessarily mean that they are in financial trouble! Many organisations manage perfectly well with net current liabilities, or negative working capital. In a later chapter we will look at how this can happen.

Exercise

Before going on to consider each item of working capital in detail, check your understanding by calculating the value of this company's working capital.

Balances at 31 December, year 6: Cash £130, Creditors £760, Debtors £980, Stock £840, Bank overdraft £320.

Solution

Current assets = £130 + £980 + £840 = £1,950

Current liabilities = £760 + £320 = £1,080

Working capital = net current assets = £1,950 – £1,080 = £870.

Remember that this is the working capital balance only at the balance sheet date. It might have been totally different one day before and will almost certainly be different in one month's time.

3.5.3 Current assets: stock

In Figure 3.1 there were three types of stock: raw materials, work in progress and finished goods. Valuing these stocks for the balance sheet involves some subjective judgement. This will become obvious as we now discuss each type of stock in turn.

Raw materials stock

For example, consider the case of the raw materials purchased by your plant pot business. Suppose that, at the year end, the business was holding a number of containers of paint in stock which need to be valued. A logical way to value them might be to look up the invoices and find out how much was paid for them. This is in fact the recommended accounting practice (from Statement of Standard Accounting Practice No. 9): 'stocks should be valued at the lower of cost and net realisable value.'

Net realisable value is the amount that the items can be sold for, less any amount that has to be spent to complete the sale.

But what if several batches of paint are muddled together, some of which cost £5 each, some cost £6 each, and some cost, say, £7 each. Which price should be used?

The answer is that there are two possible prices that could be used for the published accounts. Stocks can either be valued at the price of the latest items received into stock (this is the 'first in, first out' or FIFO valuation method) or they can be valued at a weighted average price of all the items in stock. Management is free to select the method that they feel is most appropriate, but once a stock valuation method is selected it must be applied consistently. It is not acceptable to continually change the stock valuation method in use.

The following extract from Whitbread plc's annual report for 1999/2000 will demonstrate how a company might explain its stock valuation policy:

'Stocks are stated at the lower of cost and net realisable value. The cost of finished goods includes appropriate overheads. Cost is calculated on the basis of first in, first out and net realisable value is the estimated selling price less any costs of disposal.'

For internal management accounting purposes any stock valuation may be used, as long as it provides information that is useful to managers.

Work in progress stock
Valuing work in progress can be even more problematic. Imagine that your business has some plant pots that have been painted, but which are awaiting finishing and packing. Following the 'lower of cost and net realisable value' rule we could value them by working out the cost incurred so far. We can determine the value of the raw materials that have gone into them, and we should be able to work out the wages incurred in making and painting them, although of course there would be some subjective judgement involved in this. We should also be able to calculate a reasonable charge for the over-head cost incurred so far (the power to run the kiln, etc.) and add this on to the total value.

In a later chapter you will be looking at how the overhead cost is determined for each item produced.

An item of work in progress would therefore have a higher value than the basic raw material, because wages and overhead costs have been incurred in beginning to convert it into a finished product.

However, if you tried to sell a part-finished plant pot it would probably be very difficult. You would almost certainly have more trouble selling it than you would if you tried to sell the untouched basic raw material. Therefore in practice the work in progress has very little value, certainly a lower value than we are placing on it. Are we overstating its value?

The point is that the business will not be trying to sell a part-finished plant pot. The intention is to incur further cost in finishing and packing the pot ready for sale. Therefore the part-finished pot has a greater **value to the business as a going concern** than the untouched raw materials. The going concern concept assumes that the business will continue in existence for the foreseeable future, therefore the assets should be valued on this basis and not on the basis of what they could be sold for if the business was broken up.

Finished goods stock

Finished goods stock is also valued at the lower of cost and net realisable value and of course its unit value will be higher than the work in progress because yet more costs will have been incurred in bringing it to the finished condition.

Notice that Whitbread plc's policy statement above explains that the cost of finished goods includes appropriate overheads.

3.5.4 Current assets: debtors

Current assets are usually arranged on a balance sheet in reverse order of liquidity, i.e. in the order of how difficult they are to turn into money.
Stock is the least liquid current asset because it is necessary to find a customer for it, and then give the customer credit, before the cash is finally received. Stock therefore appears first in the list of current assets. Next in order of liquidity comes debtors, and this balance is shown below stocks on Example plc's balance sheet.

Exercise
You have seen that the valuation of stock is subjective. Can you think of a reason why the valuation of debtors for the balance sheet might also be subjective?

Solution
Some of the debtors might not pay their bills!

Although it is fairly straightforward to work out how much money is owed to the business by its debtors, some subjective judgement is involved in determining how much of this is actually likely to be received. The business may know of certain customers who are in difficulties and will not pay. These debts can be written off as bad debts and they are not shown as a valuable asset on the balance sheet.

However, the managers may know from past experience that other customers are also unlikely to pay, but they may not be able to pinpoint which specific customers these are. Therefore it is common practice to make a provision for doubtful debts in addition to writing off the definite bad debts.

Exercise

X Limited has debtor balances of £34,500 at the year end. Included in these balances is a customer who owes £5,500 but who has gone into liquidation, informing X Limited that he is unlikely to be able to settle any of the outstanding debt. After writing off this debt, X Limited wishes to make a general provision for doubtful debts equal to one per cent of the remaining balances.

What amount should be shown for debtors on X Limited's balance sheet?

Solution

General provision for doubtful debts = 1% x (£34,500 – £5,500) = £290

Debtors balance for balance sheet = £34,500 – £5,500 – £290 = £28,710

3.5.5 Current assets: prepayments

In Chapter 2 we saw how the charge to the profit and loss account for some expenses was adjusted if payments had been made in advance. For example, if insurance has been paid in advance for the next quarter then the amount paid in advance (the prepayment) is deducted from the total paid and only the remainder is charged as an expense in the profit and loss account.

The amount of the prepayment is another form of current asset which represents value to the business: the right to continue for three months without needing to pay any more insurance costs. Prepayments are usually shown within the debtors figure in the balance sheet.

3.5.6 Current assets: cash at bank and in hand

You are probably thinking, at last, surely this is an asset which is not subjectively valued! In many cases you would be correct. But what if Example plc is holding balances of foreign currency to finance its international trading activities? At what rate should these be converted to sterling for the balance sheet?

If you have ever returned from a foreign holiday with a few banknotes to exchange you will know that the amount they are worth in sterling can vary dramatically on a daily basis. You will therefore appreciate the difficulty in valuing what could be fairly substantial holdings of foreign currency. Guidelines exist to help accountants with this task, in the form of an Accounting Standard on foreign currency translation, but there is still plenty of scope for management judgement.

Sadly, even the cash figure in the balance sheet may be the subject of considerable estimation!

3.5.7 Current liabilities

You will see that under the heading of current liabilities on Example plc's balance sheet it states 'creditors: amounts falling due within one year'. This is a clear statement of what is meant by current liabilities.

A liability is an amount of money owed by the organisation, and a **current** liability is one which is due to be paid within a year. There are many different types of creditor or current liability since, as we have already stated, a business may be able to obtain credit for almost everything. If you are an employee you may be a creditor of your organisation at the moment because they may owe you up to one month's salary, assuming that you are paid monthly and depending on the payment date. Therefore if you go into work tomorrow and your boss tells you that you are a liability, this is hopefully stated in the context that you are a current liability on your organisation's balance sheet! Before leaving our discussion of creditors we will have a look at a few common types of current liability that you may come across.

Bank loans and overdrafts

Many bank loans are for more than one year and will be shown elsewhere on the balance sheet, as you will see later. However if, say, a ten-year loan was taken out nine years ago it is now due for repayment within one year and should be shown as a current liability.

Many overdrafts are in practical terms a permanent source of finance and are effectively like a long-term loan. However, an overdraft is in reality liable to be recalled at any time. The bank manager may request that it is repaid at quite short notice. Hence it should also be classified as a current liability.

Proposed dividend

A company is a separate legal person from its shareholders. Therefore once a dividend has been proposed in the profit and loss account, this becomes a liability of the company to the shareholders until it is paid. If you look at Example plc's profit and loss account at the beginning of Chapter 2 you will see that the dividends for the year were £230,000. If these dividends have not yet been paid then they will be included in the creditors figure of £600,000 shown on Example plc's balance sheet.

It may be that part of the £230,000 dividend was paid as an interim dividend during the year. In this case only the balance remaining to be paid (the final dividend) will be included within the creditors figure.

Accruals

In Chapter 2 we saw how the charge to the profit and loss account for some expenses was adjusted if payments were still outstanding. For example, if the telephone bill for the latest quarter has not yet been paid then an estimate of the amount owing (the accrual) is added to the total paid to arrive at the amount to be charged as an expense in the profit and loss account.

The amount of the accrual is another form of current liability to be included within the creditors figure in the balance sheet.

3.5.8 The working capital cycle in non-manufacturing organisations

Non-manufacturing organisations also have a working capital cycle, but it will be slightly different from the one described above. For example, retail organisations who purchase finished goods ready for sale to the customer will not have any stocks of raw materials and work in progress. But they will still have stocks of finished goods, cash, creditors and some debtors.

Since many retail organisations, such as supermarkets, do not give credit to their customers, the debtors balance is likely to consist mostly of prepayments, as discussed in section 3.5.5.

Other types of service organisation such as a haulage company or contract cleaning service would not hold any stocks at all for sale to the customer (although they may have stocks of spare parts or cleaning materials). Most of these organisations' working capital cash goes into overheads which are incurred to provide the service for the customer. This overhead expenditure does not immediately produce a tangible asset such as stock which can be shown on the balance sheet. Instead the expenditure creates the service for the customer, who can then be shown as a debtor under current assets on the balance sheet.

3.6 Goodwill

Now that we have finished looking at all the items on one side of Example plc's balance sheet you should stop to think for a minute. Can you see that the total of the top part of this balance sheet shows the total amount of money tied up in Example's fixed assets and working capital? In very simple terms you might say that this shows the value of the business. But it does not. The business is likely to be worth far more than £3,066,000.

Exercise
Can you think of valuable assets that Example plc might possess that do not seem to be shown on the balance sheet?

Solution
Items that you might have thought of include skilled employees, customer and supplier relationships, databases and information technology systems.

If another company wanted to acquire or take over Example plc it is likely that they would have to pay a lot more than £3,066,000 to acquire the business. The extra amount that they would have to pay is called goodwill, an intangible asset.

Purchased goodwill is treated the same as a purchased tangible fixed asset. The cost of the goodwill is spread out or amortised over a number of years, usually less than twenty years. For example, the following extract is taken from Whitbread plc's statement of accounting policies for 1999/2000. It appears under the heading of 'intangible fixed assets'.

'Goodwill arising on acquisitions is capitalised. It is amortised, on a straight-line basis, over its estimated useful economic life up to a maximum of twenty years.'

Amortisation of goodwill appears as an expense in each year's profit and loss account. The balance of goodwill is held on the balance sheet as an intangible asset. This balance reduces each year by the amount of the amortisation charge.

3.7 Capitalisation of costs

When expenditure is capitalised this means that it is treated as fixed asset expenditure (capital expenditure) and is held in the balance sheet to be spread over the profit and loss accounts of several years. A cost may be treated in this way if it can be demonstrated that the expenditure incurred will provide benefit for future years.

This has the effect of increasing profits, but perhaps only in the short term since the capitalised fixed asset will usually have to be depreciated in future.

A common example is the **capitalisation of interest**. Sometimes the interest charges incurred on money borrowed to finance the construction of a fixed asset are not charged against the profit for the year. Insead the interest is added to the value of the fixed asset in the balance sheet, and the total amount will be depreciated over the estimated useful life of the relevant asset.

For example, J Sainsbury plc's annual report for 2000 details the following accounting policy:

*'**Capitalisation of interest**. Interest incurred on borrowings for the financing of specific property developments is capitalised.'*

The notes to J Sainsbury's accounts reveal that £10 million out of the total interest payable of £122 million was capitalised into the value of fixed assets, i.e. added to the fixed asset value in the balance sheet instead of being charged against the profit for the year.

Other costs which some companies may capitalise and amortise over several years include the costs of developing software or an internet site. Many companies charge these expenses to the profit and loss account in the year in which they are incurred, but in some circumstances they can be capitalised and depreciated or amortised over several years.

3.8 Capital and reserves

Now we can move on to the bottom part of the balance sheet: the part that shows where the money has come from to invest in the fixed assets and working capital.

So that you can refer to it easily, the relevant part of the balance sheet from the beginning of the chapter is repeated below.

Extract from Example plc's balance sheet as at 31 December year 7

	£000
Capital and reserves	
Called-up share capital	2,200
Reserves – retained profits	580
Shareholders' funds	2,780
Creditors falling due after more than one year	286
Capital employed	3,066

3.8.1 Share capital

We have already discussed at the beginning of Chapter 2 how the shareholders are the owners of the business – they each have a share in its fortunes. The term 'called-up' share capital in Example plc's balance sheet indicates the amount that shareholders have so far been asked to pay for their shares.

For example, a company might sell 50p shares to the public, requiring them to pay 25p immediately (the called-up capital) and the remaining 25p at a later date.

The most common types of share are preference shares and ordinary shares. Preference shares are so called because they have preference over the payment of dividends and the repayment of capital. Each year the preference shareholders will receive their dividend payment first, and any profits left will belong to the ordinary shareholders. This may be a large or small (or non-existent!) amount of money, depending on how well the company has performed during the year. However, preference shares will receive only a fixed rate of dividend. The potential dividends for ordinary shareholders are, in theory, unlimited. Another difference between the two types of share is that in the event of the company winding up, the preference shareholders' capital would be repaid before the ordinary shareholders receive any repayment.

In most cases, even the preference shareholders' dividends are not guaranteed. Dividend payments depend on the company making profits. Furthermore, remember that the company will not necessarily pay out as dividend all of the remaining profit available for the ordinary shareholders. Some of the profit will be kept as reserves to fund future growth.

3.8.2 Reserves

We saw in Chapter 2 that retained profit is an important source of finance for a company. Retained profit is one of the most common reserves that you will see in company balance sheets. The retained profits reserve balance is merely a statement of how much profit has been retained over the years to fund the company's growth. Do not make the very common mistake of thinking that the reserves balance in the shareholders' funds represents hoards of cash which the company has access to. Reserves are not cash. They are merely a source of finance that has been used to buy, say, more fixed assets or stock to increase the company's operations. The reserves figure shows where the money originally came from. If you want to know whether the company has any cash then look at the other side of the balance sheet, under current assets!

3.8.3 Shareholders' funds

The total of the shareholders' funds represents their total investment in the company. The reserves belong to the shareholders just as much as their original capital does. For example, in the case of retained profits they have effectively agreed that the company should reinvest the profits on their behalf. The profits still belong to the shareholders, but the profits are now tied up in the company's assets.

The term used to describe the ordinary share capital plus reserves is the 'equity' of the business.

3.9 Longer-term liabilities

The last item on Example plc's balance sheet is 'creditors falling due after more than one year'. The most common item within this category is loan capital. For example, money may be borrowed from a bank on a twenty-year loan. There will be a legally binding agreement to repay the loan after twenty years and to pay regular amounts of interest at agreed rates through-out the duration of the loan.

Mortgages are another form of loan that would be shown under this cat-egory, if they are due to be repaid after more than one year.

Occasionally you may come across balance sheets where the longer-term liabilities are shown as a deduction from the 'other side' of the balance sheet. If this were done for Example plc the lower part of the balance sheet would look like this:

	£000
	.....
Total assets less current liabilities	3,066
Creditors falling due after more than one year	286
	2,780
Capital and reserves	
Called-up share capital	2,200
Retained profits	580
Shareholders' funds	2,780

The principles of the balance sheet have not altered. This alternative pres-entation merely serves to highlight the shareholders' investment in the company.

Exercise

The following balances have been extracted from List Limited's accounts on 31 December:

	£
Freehold buildings	
(at valuation less accumulated depreciation)	381,000
Stock of goods for resale	87,000
Bank loan (due for repayment in ten years)	72,000
Bank overdraft	6,500
Fixtures and fittings at cost	118,000
Amount owed by customers	68,000
Share capital	390,000
Retained profit reserve	68,500
Insurance prepaid	750
Accumulated depreciation on fixtures and fittings	35,000
Wages and salaries owing	1,250
Cash in tills	200
Amount owed to suppliers	81,700

Reorganise this data to produce List Limited's balance sheet as at 31 December.

Solution

Notice how the second and third columns are used to carry out the calculations of any required subtotals.

	£	£	£
Fixed assets			
Freehold buildings (at valuation			
less accumulated depreciation)			381,000
Fixtures and fittings at cost		118,000	
less accumulated depreciation		35,000	
		83,000	
		464,000	
Current assets			
Stock		87,000	
Debtors		68,000	
Prepayments		750	
Cash		200	
		155,950	
Current liabilities			
Creditors	81,700		
Accrued expenses	1,250		
Bank overdraft	6,500		
		89,450	
Net current assets			66,500
Total assets less current liabilities			530,500
Capital and reserves			
Share capital			390,000
Retained profit			68,500
			458,500
Creditors falling due after more than one year			72,000
Capital employed			530,500

3.10 Summary

1. A balance sheet is a statement that shows the things of value that an organisation owns (the assets), as well as the sources of finance used to buy them.
2. Expenditure on fixed assets is called capital expenditure and it benefits the organisation for several years.
3. Expenditure on running costs is called revenue expenditure.
4. The depreciation charge in the profit and loss account is used to share out capital expenditure over the years that gain benefit from it.

5. Working capital is the capital that is circulating round the business. The balance of working capital is calculated as current assets minus current liabilities.
6. Net current assets is another term used to describe working capital.
7. Stocks are valued at the lower of cost and net realisable value.
8. Current liabilities are those that are due for payment within a year of the balance sheet date.
9. Goodwill is the difference between the value of the business as a whole and the value of the net assets.
10. Reserves are shown within shareholders' funds to indicate the original source of finance.

Review questions

1. What is the difference between capital expenditure and revenue expenditure? (section 3.3)
2. What are intangible fixed assets? (section 3.4.1)
3. What is the purpose of the depreciation charge in the profit and loss account? (section 3.4.3)
4. What is meant by the term 'net book value'? (section 3.4.2)
5. What are the constituent parts of net current assets? (section 3.5.2)
6. What is the going concern concept and what is its significance in terms of the valuation of stock? (section 3.5.3)
7. Where would you show prepayments in a balance sheet? (section 3.5.5)
8. What distinguishes a current liability from a non-current liability? (section 3.5.7)
9. How is goodwill calculated? (section 3.6)

Self-test questions

1. Present the following information in the form of a balance sheet as at 31 December.

	Balance at 31 December £
Accounts payable	29,700
Ordinary share capital	68,000
Delivery vehicle at net book value	12,800
Accrued expenses	1,700
Stock	70,000
Accounts receivable	26,400
Cash	1,100
Other creditors	1,800
Office equipment at net book value	8,400
Prepaid expenses	7,200
Retained profit reserve	14,700
Loan (repayable in seven years)	10,000

2. Comment critically on the following statements.

   (a) 'Charging a depreciation provision in the profit and loss account ensures we will have funds to replace the relevant fixed asset.'
   (b) 'The balance sheet measures the value of a business because it lists the values of all the assets and then deducts the liabilities to deduce the net business value.'
   (c) 'An accrued expense is one that should be charged in next year's profit and loss account.'

Answers to self-test questions

1. Balance sheet as at 31 December

	£	£	£
Fixed assets at net book value			
Office equipment			8,400
Delivery vehicle			12,800
			21,200
Current assets			
Stock		70,000	
Accounts receivable (debtors)		26,400	
Prepaid expenses		7,200	
Cash		1,100	
		104,700	
Current liabilities			
Accounts payable (creditors)	29,700		
Other creditors	1,800		
Accrued expenses	1,700		
		33,200	
Net current assets			71,500
Total assets less current liabilities			92,700
Capital and reserves			
Share capital			68,000
Retained profit reserve			14,700
			82,700
Creditors falling due after more than one year			10,000
			92,700

2.

(a) The depreciation provision is a mechanism to allocate, as fairly as possible, the cost of the asset (less any residual value) over its useful life. The depreciation provision is charged as a cost in the profit and loss account for each year, but this does not involve actually putting aside any cash for the fixed asset's replacement. Even if an amount of cash equal to the depreciation provision was set aside each year, this would still not ensure the availability of adequate funds for replacement of the asset. Inflation and technological change may mean that the replacement asset will cost more.

(b) The balance sheet does not measure the value of a business.
   (i) It does not necessarily include all the business assets. For example, only purchased goodwill may be shown on the balance sheet. Internally

generated intangible assets can only be capitalised (shown on the balance sheet) if they have a readily ascertainable market value.

(ii) Those assets which are shown are not necessarily included at their market value. For example:

- Fixed assets are shown at their net book value. This is merely the part of the original cost that has not yet been depreciated through the profit and loss account. It is not necessarily an indication of the market value of the fixed assets.
- Stocks are valued at the lower of cost and net realisable value. The cost includes subjective elements such as an amount of allocated overhead.
- Debtors are stated net of a provision for doubtful debts, which may be too high or too low.

(iii) Some of the liabilities which are included may be estimates, for example the accrued expenses.

(c) An accrued expense is charged in the current year's profit and loss account. It is an expense which should be matched with the current year's revenue, but which has not yet been paid. It will appear as a current liability in the balance sheet.

Cash-flow reporting

4.1 Introduction

In this chapter you will find out about the importance of cash flow. We will be looking at the published cash-flow statement and the internal document which is used to monitor cash flow: the cash-flow forecast.

4.2 The importance of cash flow

Suppose that one morning you wake up with the most brilliant idea for a business. You cannot believe your luck in that nobody else has thought of it and it is obviously an absolute winner! There is no doubt that if you embark on this venture then you will be a millionaire by Christmas. The only problem is that you will need plenty of capital, and your savings will not be sufficient.

Undaunted, you ring your bank manager to arrange an appointment to negotiate a loan. You are told that the manager will be leaving for an extended holiday that afternoon, but that you can be seen this morning. Otherwise you will have to wait for two weeks and that will be too late – somebody else will get into the market before you!

So you jump into the car and drive towards the bank in plenty of time for your appointment. Then you notice that you do not have enough petrol to reach town so you stop at the petrol station. A big notice states 'Please do not put petrol into your vehicle if you do not have the means to pay'. At this point you realise that in your rush to leave the house you did not pick up any money or your credit cards. So what can you do?

You do not have enough petrol to go back home, you cannot reach the bank on foot and you have no money for a bus or a taxi. You could try negotiating with the petrol station cashier, offering vast sums of money for a tank of petrol, with the promise that you will pay this afternoon, once you have seen the bank manager. You could try approaching the other people in the queue.

But these people are unlikely to help you. They do not know who you are, they have only your word for it that you are on your way to being a millionaire. Therefore you are stuck and your business is stopped before it has even started. A potentially profitable venture has failed because of a lack of cash planning. If you had stopped and thought ahead about the fact that you would need cash part-way through your journey you could have made plans to cover the cash deficit – you would have picked up some cash before you left!

This may seem like an oversimplification, but it is what is happening to businesses every day. An otherwise sound, potentially profitable business can fail due to what might be a temporary cash problem, because nobody is willing to take the risk and advance them the cash that they need to continue.

Cash planning and cash management are therefore vital to the success and survival of every business.

4.3 Cash-flow statements

4.3.1 Cash-flow information

In addition to a profit and loss account and balance sheet, companies are required to include in their annual report a cash-flow statement. This enables the users of accounts to assess the amounts, timing and uncertainty of the organisation's cash flows. Where does the organisation get cash from? What large cash movements have there been during the year? The profit and loss account shows how much profit has been earned, but this does not necessarily mean that the organisation will have any cash.

Exercise

Can you think of a few reasons why an organisation might be making profits, but still be very short of cash?

Solution

There are many varied reasons that you might have suggested, including:

1. Profits may have been reinvested into building up stocks in anticipation of a sales drive.
2. Although sales have been made and are included in the profit and loss account as turnover (and therefore a profit on the sale is shown), the customers may not yet have paid. Therefore the cash is tied up in debtors.
3. Cash may have been invested in fixed assets. This represents a drain on cash, but the cost is not charged immediately to the profit and loss account. Only a proportion of the cost is charged as depreciation. Therefore, profits can be relatively high when cash balances are low.

4.3.2 Cash-flow statement – an example

Cash flows are presented under a number of main headings, some of which are shown in the following cash-flow statement for Example plc.

Example plc: cash-flow statement for the year ended 31 December year 7

	£000
Net cash inflow from operating activities	590
Returns on investments and servicing of finance	(40)
Corporation tax paid	(125)
Capital expenditure	(180)
	245
Equity dividends paid	(200)
Net cash inflow before financing	45
Financing	(20)
Increase in cash	25

Now we will look at each of these items in turn.

Net cash inflow from operating activities
This is the cash generated by Example plc's everyday activities, which you will by now appreciate is not the same as the profit earned during the year. Basically this figure can be calculated by determining the *cash* received from customers during the year (which is not the same as the sales made) and then deducting the *cash* paid for supplies and other services.

Because of a possible build-up of stocks, and the time delays caused by credit payments, the cash paid to suppliers etc. will not be the same as the amount charged in the profit and loss account.

Returns on investments and servicing of finance
Included under this heading would be the interest paid out to the suppliers of Example's loan capital.

Corporation tax paid
This is the actual cash paid to the tax authorities during the year. This is not the same as the taxation charge in the profit and loss account because of the timing of tax payments.

Capital expenditure
The cash flows arising from the purchase and sale of fixed assets will be shown under this heading. As you have already seen, the purchase of fixed assets can lead to some very large cash outflows.

Equity dividends paid

The dividends paid to Example plc's ordinary shareholders would be shown here. Note this is not necessarily the same as the dividend proposed for the year because of the timing of cash payments.

Financing

These are the cash flows arising from the providers of capital. Items under this heading would include cash inflows from the sale of shares and the issue of loans, and cash outflows from the repayment of long-term loans and share capital.

The statement therefore shows the cash flows that have resulted in the change in the cash balance over the year. You will learn how to interpret cash-flow statements in Chapter 7.

4.4 Cash forecasts

The cash-flow statement in the annual accounts helps people outside the company to monitor the cash-generating ability of the organisation. However, this statement will be of little assistance to managers internal to the business when they are trying to ensure that the business does not run into cash problems in the future, i.e. when they are trying to ensure that they do not get stuck at the petrol pumps!

For planning cash requirements in the future an internal planning document is used which is called the cash forecast. This is one of the most important financial planning documents in a business. It will show the cash effect of all the decisions taken in the planning process: management decisions are taken every day concerning factors such as stockholding policy and credit policy. As you have seen, these decisions will all affect cash flow.

These decisions may be designed to maximise the profitability of the organisation, but if there are insufficient cash resources to finance the plans they may need to be modified, or action might be needed to alleviate the cash restraint.

 The cash-flow forecast is referred to as an internal planning document because it is not usually made available to people outside the business.

A cash forecast can give forewarning of potential cash problems so that managers can be prepared for the situation and not be caught unawares.

There are four possible cash positions that could arise:

Cash position	Possible management action
Short-term deficit	Arrange a bank overdraft, reduce debtors and stocks, increase creditors.
Long-term deficit	Raise long-term finance, such as a loan or share capital.
Short-term surplus	Invest short term, increase debtors and stocks to boost sales, pay creditors early to obtain a cash discount.
Long-term surplus	Expand or diversify operations, replace or update fixed assets.

 A business that is permanently short of cash is not necessarily doomed. It may be that it simply needs more long-term capital to finance an increased level of activity.

You can see that the type of action taken by management will depend not only on whether a surplus or deficit is expected but also on how long the situation is expected to last. For instance, there would be little point in raising a long-term loan to cover a deficit which is expected to last for only three months.

The efficient manager must ensure that there is ample warning of both factors:

- Will there be cash surpluses or deficits?
- For how long will the surpluses or deficits last?

The cash forecast can provide the necessary warning. It is a statement which shows for each period in the near future (this could be months, weeks, or even days) the forecast cash receipts and payments, and the resulting forecast cash balances.

For example, a cash forecast might look like this:

	Jan £000	Feb £000	Mar £000	Apr £000	May £000	Jun £000
Receipts						
Sales	100	120	180	165	140	150
Other	10	10	10	10	10	10
Total receipts	110	130	190	175	150	160
Payments						
Material	65	90	80	55	60	55
Labour	50	50	50	50	50	50
Overheads	40	40	40	40	40	40
Purchase of office equipment	–	80	–	–	–	–
Total payments	155	260	170	145	150	145
Net cash flow	(45)	(130)	20	30	–	15
Opening cash balance	115	70	(60)	(40)	(10)	(10)
Closing cash balance	70	(60)	(40)	(10)	(10)	5

For each type of receipt and payment the cash flow is forecast to give the forecast net cash flow for the month. Looking at the January column, the forecast cash inflow is £110,000. The forecast cash outflow is £155,000 which results in a net cash outflow for January of £45,000 (£155,000 – £110,000). Based on the estimated cash flows between the date that the forecast is prepared and the beginning of January, the forecast opening cash balance in January is £115,000. This means that the forecast closing cash balance for January is £70,000 (£115,000 – £45,000). This becomes the opening balance for February, and so on to the end of June.

Managers using this cash forecast will be able to see that they will need short-term overdraft facilities from February until May. Alternatively, they could revise some of the planning decisions that they have taken, for example they could alter their proposed stock or credit policy. However, if you look within the figures in the cash forecast, you can see that the main item causing the short-term deficit is the purchase of office equipment in February. If this item was removed from the forecast then no deficit would arise at all.

- Perhaps the purchase of the equipment could be delayed until June, when sufficient cash will be available?
- Could credit facilities be negotiated?
- Could the equipment be leased instead of purchased outright? This would improve the cash-flow situation.

The important point is that the cash-flow forecast has forewarned managers that a cash deficit will arise if they proceed as planned. They can take action in plenty of time to cover the deficit, or to avoid it arising.

Exercise
Based on the above cash forecast, what level of overdraft facility would you recommend?

Solution
The answer is not simply to look along the bottom line of closing cash balances and assume that the overdraft requirement is £60,000, i.e. the highest month-end overdrawn balance. It is important to consider the possible timing of cash flows within each month. For example in March, the opening balance is forecast to be £60,000 negative. If all the payments in March happen before any receipts come in, then the possible overdrawn balance could be as high as £60,000 + £170,000, or £230,000 negative.

This extreme situation is unlikely to arise, but it is possible that the timing of cash flows during the month could result in an overdraft greater than £60,000. Therefore it is important to look within the figures when interpreting the information provided by a cash forecast.

4.5 Profit and loss, cash flow and balance sheet: an example

To conclude this chapter there now follows a worked example which will draw on everything you have learned so far. Work through the example carefully and ensure that you understand where each figure in the solution has come from.

S and P Catering Limited
Sheila and Paul have recently been made redundant from their jobs in the company which employed them both. They have decided to use their redundancy money to set up a catering business. Since they intend to expand the business and seek investment from their friends and family in the future, they have decided to create a limited company, S and P Catering Limited.

Their business will offer a mobile catering service to offices, shops, pubs and factory premises in the local area. Hot meals, salads and sandwiches will be prepared in the business premises and then delivered to customers in insulated containers.

Sheila and Paul have already identified a ready market for their service and the business will commence trading on 1 July. They have approached their bank to negotiate overdraft facilities for the company and the bank manager has asked them to produce a forecast profit and loss account, cash-flow statement and balance sheet for the first six months of trading.

This is the sort of information that would be required to present to the bank manager when you go to discuss a loan for your brilliant business idea.

They have spent a lot of time in preparing the forecasts below, but they have no idea how to produce the statements which their bank manager has requested.

They have asked you to help them by preparing the required statements. Sheila and Paul have provided you with the following forecasts.

1. **Capital**

   The initial share capital will consist of Sheila and Paul's redundancy money of £8,000 each.

2. **Forecast sales**

	£
July	7,500
August	8,750
September	10,750
October	11,000
November	11,500
December	11,500
	61,000

   Eighty per cent of the sales will be paid for immediately in cash. The remainder will be made on credit, payable one month later.

3. **Fixed assets**

   (a) Equipment will be purchased on 1 July for £4,000 cash. The equipment is expected to have a ten-year life with no residual value after ten years.

   (b) Two second-hand delivery vehicles will also be purchased for cash on 1 July for £6,000 each. They are expected to last for three years, after which time they will have no value.

4. **Ingredients**

   All ingredients will be purchased as they are required and no stocks will be held. Although Sheila hopes to negotiate a credit agreement once the business has got going, initially they will have to pay cash for all ingredients.

Ingredients will be purchased as follows:

	£
July	2,525
August	2,775
September	2,685
October	2,745
November	3,335
December	3,335
	17,400

5. *Packing materials*

Packing materials will be purchased as follows:

	£
July	3,300
August	1,060
September	1,305
October	1,335
November	1,395
December	1,405
	9,800

Credit arrangements have been negotiated and the suppliers will require payment one month after the purchases are made.

Stocks of packing materials are expected to amount to £2,400 at the end of December.

6. *Salaries*
Paul and Sheila will each be paid salaries of £1,500 per month. A part-time driver will be paid £400 per month.

7. *Overheads*
(a) The business premises will be rented for £600 per month, payable quarterly in advance.
(b) Rates will amount to £1,200 per annum. This will be paid in two equal instalments on 1 July and 31 December.
(c) Expenses for telephones, gas and electricity will amount to £350 for the quarter ending 30 September. This will be paid in cash in October. These expenses for the quarter ending 31 December will be £600, which will be paid in cash next January.
(d) £180 per month is to be allowed for sundry cash expenses.

(e) Insurance of £800 will be paid on 1 July to cover the twelve-month period ending 30 June of the following year.

(f) Advertising expenses of £440 will be incurred in cash in July. From August onwards, a continuous advertisement will be placed in a number of local newspapers for a monthly cost of £150, to be paid in cash.

8. *Dividend*

Sheila and Paul intend to propose an interim dividend of £2,000 on 31 December, to be paid in cash on 31 March of the following year.

9. *Taxation and interest*

Ignore taxation, VAT and PAYE, and the interest cost of any overdraft.

Solution

The figures in brackets refer to the explanatory notes at the end of the solution.

Notice that the third column is used to perform a separate calculation for packing materials.

S and P Catering Limited: forecast profit and loss account for the six months ending 31 December

	£	£	£
Sales revenue (1)			61,000
less			
Ingredients cost		17,400	
Packing materials purchases (2)	9,800		
less closing stock (3)	2,400		
		7,400	
Salaries (4)		20,400	
Rent (5)		3,600	
Rates (6)		600	
Telephone etc. (7)		950	
Sundry (8)		1,080	
Insurance (9)		400	
Advertising (10)		1,190	
Depreciation:			
equipment (11)		200	
vehicles (12)		2,000	
			55,220
Profit for the period			5,780
Dividend (13)			2,000
Retained profit to reserves			3,780

S and P Catering Limited: cash-flow forecast for the six months ending 31 December

	Jul £	Aug £	Sep £	Oct £	Nov £	Dec £
Receipts						
Share capital	16,000					
Cash sales (14)	6,000	7,000	8,600	8,800	9,200	9,200
Credit sales (15)		1,500	1,750	2,150	2,200	2,300
Total receipts	22,000	8,500	10,350	10,950	11,400	11,500
Payments						
Equipment (16)	4,000					
Vehicles	12,000					
Ingredients	2,525	2,775	2,685	2,745	3,335	3,335
Packing (17)		3,300	1,060	1,305	1,335	1,395
Salaries	3,400	3,400	3,400	3,400	3,400	3,400
Rent	1,800			1,800		
Rates	600					600
Telephone etc. (18)				350		
Sundry	180	180	180	180	180	180
Insurance	800					
Advertising	440	150	150	150	150	150
Total payments	25,745	9,805	7,475	9,930	8,400	9,060
Net cash flow (19)	(3,745)	(1,305)	2,875	1,020	3,000	2,440
Opening balance (20)		(3,745)	(5,050)	(2,175)	(1,155)	1,845
Closing balance	(3,745)	(5,050)	(2,175)	(1,155)	1,845	4,285

S and P Catering Limited: forecast balance sheet as at 31 December

	£	£	£
Fixed assets			
Equipment at cost	4,000		
less depreciation	200		
		3,800	
Vehicles at cost	12,000		
less depreciation	2,000		
		10,000	
Total fixed assets			13,800
Current assets			
Stock		2,400	
Debtors (21)		2,300	
Prepaid expenses:			
rates (22)		600	
insurance (23)		400	
Bank (24)		4,285	
		9,985	
Current liabilities			
Creditors (25)	1,405		
Accrued expenses:			
telephone etc. (26)	600		
Proposed dividend (27)	2,000		
		4,005	
Net current assets			5,980
			19,780
Capital and reserves			
Share capital			16,000
Reserves – retained profit (28)			3,780
			19,780

Note that the company is forecast to make profits over the six months, but that in the short term they will have a cash deficit for which arrangements must be made.

Explanatory notes
1. Even though some of the sales are made on credit, all the sales revenue for the period is shown in the profit and loss account.
2. Similarly, all the packing material purchases are shown, even though some of the purchases will not yet have been paid for.

3. It would not be fair to charge against sales the cost of all purchases made in the period, because some of the packing materials will still be in stock. Therefore the cost of stock is deducted to arrive at the true cost of the packing materials actually used up in the period.

4. Salaries = [(£1,500 x 2) + £400] x 6 months = £20,400

5. Rent = £600 x 6 = £3,600

6. Rates for six months = $£1,200/_2$ = £600

7. Telephone etc. = £350 + £600 = £950

8. Sundry expenses = £180 x 6 = £1,080

9. Insurance for six months = $£800/_2$ = £400

10. Advertising = £440 + (£150 x 5) = £1,190

11. Depreciation for one year = $£4,000/_{10}$ = £400. Therefore depreciation for six months = £200

12. Depreciation for one year = $£12,000/_3$ = £4,000. Therefore depreciation for six months = £2,000

13. Interim dividend is paid part-way through the year, pending a final dividend payment at the end of the year (not known in this case).

14. Cash sales receipts in July = £7,500 x 80% = £6,000, and so on for the remaining months.

15. Credit sales receipts in July = nil, because these customers take one month to pay. They will pay in August, i.e. £7,500 x 20% = £1,500, and so on for the remaining months.

16. All the fixed assets are purchased on 1 July, representing an immediate cash flow.

17. No payments will be made for packing materials in July because purchases are on one month's credit. July's packing materials will be paid for in August, and so on.

18. The £600 to be paid next January for telephone, etc. does not feature in the cash forecast, because it is not a cash flow that will arise in this six-month period.

19. The forecast net cash flow for July is £22,000 inflow less £25,745 outflow, i.e. £3,725 net outflow, and so on for the remaining months.

20. The opening cash balance for July is zero because this is a new business. The closing balance from July becomes the opening balance for August, and so on.

21. Debtors will consist of December's credit customers who will not yet have paid, i.e. £11,500 x 20% = £2,300

22. The rates for the second half year will have been paid by 31 December. These will represent a payment in advance or prepayment.

23. The insurance for the full year will have been paid but only half has been charged to the profit and loss account for six months. The remaining half is a prepayment.

24. The forecast bank balance is the closing balance for December taken from the cash-flow forecast.

25. The packing material purchased in December will not have been paid for since it will be on one month's credit.

26. The £600 expenses for the quarter ending 31 December have been charged as a valid cost in the profit and loss account for the six months. However, they will not yet have been paid by the end of December therefore they must be shown as a current liability.

27. The dividend will have been proposed but not yet paid by the end of December, thus creating a liability of the company to the shareholders.

28. This is the retained profit figure shown in the profit and loss account.

It might be a good idea to return in a day or two and attempt this example without looking at the solution. Good luck!

4.6 Summary

1. A business can be making profits but still experience cash-flow problems because of the timing of receipts and payments.

2. A cash-flow statement enables people outside the business to make judgements about its ability to generate and manage cash.

3. A cash forecast is an internal planning document. It forewarns management of the cash effect of the decisions that they have taken in the planning process.

Review questions

1. In a cash-flow statement, which items are included under the heading 'financing'? (section 4.3.2)

2. What four possible cash positions could be signalled by a cash forecast? (section 4.4)

Self-test questions

1. Your friend has recently commented to you, 'I can't understand it. My accountant tells me I have made a £60,000 profit this year, but my cash balance has actually fallen by £10,000. How can this happen?'
   Prepare an explanation for your friend.

2. For each of the events below, state whether it will have:
   • a positive impact on cash flow
   • a negative impact of cash flow, or
   • no impact on cash flow

(a) An increase in debtors
(b) Depreciation of a fixed asset
(c) A reduction in creditors
(d) Write off of a bad debt
(e) An issue of ordinary shares
(f) Declaration of the ordinary dividend for the latest financial year

 3. On 1 January , AB Limited will be formed with a share capital of £150,000.
   You are asked to use the following information to produce:
   • A forecast profit and loss account for the first six months.
   • A cash-flow forecast for each of the first six months.
   • A forecast balance sheet as at 30 June, Year 1.
   (a) £95,000 will be invested immediately in fixed assets.
   (b) Sales will be generated as follows:

	£
January	120,000
February	130,000
March	135,000
April	180,000
May	200,000
June	200,000
	965,000

   (c) All sales will be made on one month's credit.
   (d) Purchases of materials for which one month's credit will be allowed:

	£
January	80,000
February	75,000
March	60,000
April	70,000
May	70,000
June	70,000
	425,000

   (e) It is expected that £75,000 of this material will still be in stock at
   the end of June, but that there will be no work-in-progress or
   finished goods stock.
   (f) Labour costs will be paid as incurred, amounting to £270,000
   incurred in even amounts over the six-month period.

(g) Overhead expenditure will be paid as follows.

	£
January	65,000
February	33,000
March	32,000
April	48,000
May	31,000
June	31,000
	240,000

Included in the January payment is an insurance bill for £20,000 which will provide cover for the whole of the year ending 31 December. Furthermore the rent bill of £8,000 for the period 1 April to 30 June will be outstanding at the end of June and is not included in the above figures.

(h) Depreciation on the fixed assets will be £3,000 for the six months.

Answers to self-test questions

1. A number of factors such as the following could have caused the cash balance to fall, despite a profit being earned.

- Fixed assets may have been purchased. This would reduce the cash balance but only a proportion of the cost would be charged against profit, in the form of a depreciation provision.
- Stocks may have increased. This would reduce cash but if the stock is unused it would not yet have been charged as an expense in the profit and loss account.
- Sales may have been made on credit. The profit would have been increased by the sale, but no cash inflow would yet have resulted.
- A loan may have been repaid. This would reduce the cash balance but would not be shown as an expense in the profit and loss account.
- Certain expenses may have been paid in advance for the next accounting period. The cash balance would have reduced but the expense would have been carried forward to be matched against the revenue for the forthcoming period.

2. (a) An increase in debtors would have a negative impact on cash flow.
   (b) Depreciation provisions have no impact on cash flow. The cash is paid out when the fixed asset is originally purchased.
   (c) A reduction in creditors would have a negative impact on cash flow.
   (d) Writing off a bad debt has no impact on cash flow.

(e) An issue of ordinary shares will have a positive impact on cash flow.

(f) Declaration of a dividend will have no impact on cash flow. The dividend proposed will be a liability of the company to the shareholders until it is paid.

3. The figures in brackets refer to the notes at the end of the solution.

AB Limited
Forecast profit and loss account for the six months ended 30 June, Year 1

	£000	£000
Sales turnover		965
Less: Materials	425	
Less stock (1)	75	
	350	
Labour	270	
Overhead (2)	238	
Depreciation	3	
		861
Profit to reserves (3)		104

AB Limited
Cash-flow forecast for the six months ended 30 June, Year 1

	Jan £000	Feb £000	Mar £000	Apr £000	May £000	Jun £000
Receipts						
Share capital	150	-	-	-	-	-
Sales receipts (4)	-	120	130	135	180	200
Total receipts	150	120	130	135	180	200
Payments						
Fixed assets	95					
Materials (5)	-	80	75	60	70	70
Labour	45	45	45	45	45	45
Overhead (6)	65	33	32	48	31	31
Total payments	205	158	152	153	146	146
Net cash flow	(55)	(38)	(22)	(18)	34	54
Opening cash balance (7)	-	(55)	(93)	(115)	(133)	(99)
Closing cash balance	(55)	(93)	(115)	(133)	(99)	(45)

AB Limited
Forecast balance sheet as at 30 June, Year 1

	£000	£000	£000
Fixed assets at cost			95
Less depreciation			3
			92
Current assets			
Material stock	75		
Debtors (8)	200		
Prepaid expenses (9)	10	285	
Less current liabilities			
Creditors (10)	70		
Accrued expenses (11)	8		
Bank overdraft (12)	45	123	
Working capital (net current assets)			162
			254
Financed by:			
Share capital			150
Reserves – retained profit (13)			104
			254

Explanatory notes
1. The stock will not have been sold therefore it should not be charged as a cost against the revenue for the period.
2.

	£000
Expenditure incurred	240
Less insurance paid in advance (£20,000 x $^6/_{12}$)	(10)
Plus rent accrued, 1st April to 30th June	8
	238

3. There will probably be some interest and tax to be paid or provided for and possibly a dividend will be declared. However there is no mention of this in the example data, so for now the balance of profit will be taken to reserves.
4. All sales will be made on one month's credit, therefore the sales for January will be received in cash in February, and so on.
5. One month's credit is allowed on material purchases, therefore the material received in January will be paid for in cash in February, and so on.
6. Overhead cash payments are detailed in the example data. The £8,000 owing for rent will not be paid in cash during this period.
7. The opening cash balance for January is zero because this is a new business.

8. The customers for June will not have paid by the end of June and they represent the debtors balance at the balance sheet date.
9. The prepaid insurance is an unused asset at the end of June.
10. AB Limited will not have paid for June materials therefore these suppliers represent the creditors balance at the balance sheet date.
11. The £8,000 rent owing is a current liability at the end of June.
12. The bank overdraft is the closing balance for June as shown on the cash-flow forecast.
13. The reserve balance is the profit transferred at the end of June as shown on the forecast profit and loss account.

5
The accounts of
not-for-profit organisations

5.1 Introduction

In this chapter we will be looking at the accounts of organisations that are not set up to make a profit, for example clubs, societies and charities. We will be assuming that you have already studied the preceding chapters on profit and loss accounts, balance sheets and cash flow statements. You will see that most of the principles in the accounts of not-for-profit organisations are exactly the same as the principles covered in these earlier chapters.

Even if your interest is focused on the accounts of profit-making organisations this chapter will provide some useful revision of the basic concepts underlying financial statements. The exercise in the chapter will also give you further practice in their application.

5.2 The differences in the accounts of not-for-profit organisations

The accounts for not-for-profit organisations are prepared in the same way as those for profit-making organisations. For example, the accruals principle is followed. You should recall that this means that expenses are only charged against revenue (or income) if they represent a fair cost for the period, and only the revenue that relates to the period is shown in that period's accounts.

Furthermore, expenditure in the accounts of not-for-profit organisations is divided between capital expenditure and revenue expenditure. The capital expenditure is apportioned over the accounts of several accounting periods, using the depreciation methods that were demonstrated in Chapter 3. The following extract from the Accounting Policies section of the charity Oxfam's accounts for 1999-2000 provides an example of this.

 Oxfam is a UK-based charity whose main aims are to relieve poverty, distress and suffering in any part of the world and to educate the public concerning the nature, causes and effects of poverty.

'Depreciation of tangible fixed assets

Freehold land is not depreciated.

The cost of other tangible fixed assets is written off by equal annual instalments over their expected useful lives as follows:

Freehold buildings	50 years
Leasehold warehouse	10 years
...	...
Furniture, fixtures and equipment overseas	3 years'

Just to refresh your memory of some of the principles covered in Chapter 3, it will be useful to have a look at the wording of parts of this statement.

- 'Freehold land is not depreciated'. It is generally accepted that land values do not depreciate.
- 'The cost of other tangible fixed assets is written off ... .' Written off in this context means to share out the original cost of the asset over the years that benefit from its use, i.e., over the fixed asset's 'expected useful life'. The cost of the asset is not charged in full as expenditure in the year in which it is purchased. Instead it is **capitalised**, i.e. taken to the balance sheet, and is charged more gradually as expenditure over the asset's useful life. A depreciation charge is made in each year's income and expenditure account (the not-for-profit organisation's equivalent of a profit and loss account).
- '... by equal annual instalments ...' means that Oxfam is using the straight-line method of depreciation, which we demonstrated in Chapter 3.

Hopefully you are beginning to appreciate that the same principles that you learned about in earlier chapters do indeed apply to not-for-profit organisations. However, there are some differences in the financial statements which are prepared for not-for-profit organisations:

(a) Since these organisations do not exist to make profits, a profit and loss account is not appropriate. Instead an **income and expenditure account** is prepared, following the same principles as a profit and loss account. This account lists separately all the items of income and expenditure, showing the net difference between the totals.

(b) The difference between income and expenditure for the period is referred to as a surplus or deficit, rather than a profit or loss.

(c) Not-for-profit organisations produce a balance sheet which shows on one side the fixed assets, current assets and current liabilities. However, because these organisations are funded differently, they will not show 'capital' or 'shareholders' funds' on the other side of the balance sheet. The capital account is replaced by an 'accumulated fund' or 'reserves'.

 The fixed assets will be shown at net book value and the current assets will be valued in the same way as for profit-making organisations. For example, any stock is valued at the lower of cost and net realisable value, and a provision will be made for any doubtful debts.

(d) The accumulated fund or reserves are carried forward in the accounts to finance the activities of future periods. Sometimes part of the fund is earmarked for specific uses and transfers may be made to separate reserves, such as the maintenance reserve to provide for maintenance work to be carried out over a number of years.

You will see from the following example that there are many similarities between the accounts of not-for-profit organisations and those of profit-making organisations.

The Managers Club: income and expenditure account for year 5

	£	£
Income		
Fees and subscriptions (note1)		40,800
Investment income		460
Income from magazine – advertising and sales		5,750
		47,010
Expenditure (note 2)		
Salaries	9,760	
Magazine costs	27,870	
Depreciation of fixed assets	1,500	
Other expenses	950	
		40,080
Surplus transferred to accumulated fund		6,930

Notes
1. All the income for the year is shown whether or not it has actually been received. Any income received in advance (e.g. advance subscriptions) is not shown in this year's income and expenditure account: it is instead carried forward on the balance sheet as a liability.
2. The expenses are adjusted for accruals and prepayments, in the same way as for a profit-making organisation

The Managers Club: balance sheet as at the end of year 5

	£	£	£
Fixed assets			
Office equipment (at cost			
less depreciation)			7,500
Investments			5,000
			12,500
Current assets			
Stock		320	
Debtors		400	
Cash at bank		900	
		1,620	
Current liabilities			
Creditors	1,020		
Salaries owing	520		
		1,540	
Net current assets			80
Net assets			12,580
Accumulated fund/reserves			12,580

The balance sheet shows that the assets held by the Managers Club have been financed by accumulated surpluses of £12,580.

These assets comprise fixed assets held at a net book value of £12,500 and net current assets (or working capital) of £80.

Exercise

Using the Managers Club's income and expenditure account as a guide to the type of activities that they undertake, can you think of examples of the items that might be included in the following figures in this organisation's balance sheet?

(i) Stock

(ii) Debtors

(iii) Creditors

Solution

You might have thought of the following:

(i) Stock: stock of magazines, and advertising and recruitment literature

(ii) Debtors: credit customers for sales of the magazines; payments due from organisations who have placed advertisements in the magazine; members' subscriptions for year 5 still outstanding at the end of the year

(iii) Creditors: outstanding bill for magazine printing costs; members' subscriptions for year 6 paid in advance

You might have thought of many other items to include under these headings, following the principles that you have learned in this and earlier chapters.

You should now be in a position to prepare a set of accounts for a not-for-profit organisation. This exercise will also provide useful practice at applying the fundamental concepts underlying the preparation of financial statements for all types of organisation.

Exercise

The following balances have been extracted from the books of the Sporting Tennis Club as at the end of year 7. Use these balances, and the notes which follow, to prepare an income and expenditure account for year 7 and a balance sheet as at the end of year 7.

	£
Subscriptions received	1,600
Utilities (gas, electricity, etc.)	375
Insurance	280
Maintenance	322
Equipment at cost	2,500
Depreciation on equipment to end of year 6	1,000
Other expenses	108
Profit from Christmas dance	380
Cash at bank	125
Fund/reserves at end of year 6	730

Notes to be taken into account
1. A further £350 of subscriptions is in arrears, i.e. these members have not yet paid their subscriptions for year 7. All these are expected to pay early in year 8. There were no arrears at the end of year 6.
2. A gas bill of £145 has been received but not yet paid. No other utility bills are outstanding.
3. Insurance of £75 has been paid in advance for year 8.
4. Equipment is depreciated on a straight-line basis over five years.

Solution

The figures in brackets refer to the explanatory notes which follow at the end of the solution.

The Sporting Tennis Club: income and expenditure account for year 7

	£	£
Income		
Subscriptions (1)		1,950
Profit from Christmas dance		380
		2,330
Expenditure		
Utilities (2)	520	
Insurance (3)	205	
Maintenance	322	
Depreciation on equipment (4)	500	
Other expenses	108	
		1,655
Surplus to reserves		675

The Sporting Tennis Club: balance sheet as at the end of year 7

	£	£
Fixed assets		
Equipment (at cost less depn.) (4)		1,000
Current assets		
Debtors (1)	350	
Prepaid expenses (3)	75	
Cash at bank	125	
	550	
Current liabilities		
Accrued expenses (2)	145	
Net current assets		405
		1,405
Accumulated fund (5)		1,405

Explanatory notes

1. The subscriptions for the year on an accruals basis are £1,600 received plus £350 still to be received in respect of year 7. The £350 outstanding is shown as a debtor under current assets on the balance sheet.
2. Utilities expense = £375 paid plus £145 accrued = £520. The £145 accrual is shown under current liabilities on the balance sheet.
3. Insurance expenses = £280 paid less £75 paid in advance = £205. The £75 relates to year 8 and should not be charged in this year's income and expenditure account. It is shown under current assets in the balance sheet.
4. The equipment cost should not be charged in the income and expenditure account because it is to be apportioned over a number of years using the depreciation charge. Annual depreciation = $£2,500/_5$ = £500. The net book value to be shown in the balance sheet is calculated as follows.

Equipment at cost	£2,500
less: depreciation to end of year 6	(£1,000)
depreciation for year 7	(£500)
Net book value at end of year 7	£1,000

5. Balance on accumulated fund at end of year 7:

Balance at end of year 6	£730
Surplus added for year 7	£675
	£1,405

How did you get on? That was quite a tough exercise and if you were able to follow its logic then you are now in a good position to move on and learn the basics of the interpretation of financial statements.

5.3 Summary

1. In a not-for-profit organisation an income and expenditure account replaces the profit and loss account that would be prepared in a profit-making organisation.
2. The main difference that arises in the balance sheet is in depicting the way in which the organisation is financed.

Review questions
1. How is capital expenditure treated in the accounts of not-for-profit organisations? (section 5.2)
2. If expenditure exceeds income for a period in a not-for-profit organisation this is not referred to as a loss. What term is used instead? (section 5.2)

Self-test questions

1. The Mother and Toddler Club received £780 in subscriptions from members during year 4, which included £90 in arrears for year 3. At the end of year 4 the members' subscriptions outstanding were £60, all of which were received early in year 5.

What are the correct entries in respect of members' subscriptions in the:

(a) income and expenditure account for year 4?
(b) balance sheet as at the end of year 4?

2. In its statement of accounting policies, Oxfam states that 'vehicles and equipment used in operational programmes are not capitalised but are charged in full to direct charitable expenditure when purchased.'

Explain:

(a) what is meant by this statement;
(b) why Oxfam may have decided not to capitalise these items.

Answers to self-test questions

1. (a) The income and expenditure account for year 4 will show, in the income section, members' subscriptions for the year of £750. This is calculated as follows.

	£
Received during year 4	780
Less amount relating to year 3	(90)
Plus year 4 subscriptions outstanding	60
	750

(b) The balance sheet as at the end of year 4 will include a current asset of £60 in respect of members' subscriptions receivable.

2. (a) If an asset is capitalised it is classified as a fixed asset and its cost is not charged in full against the income of the period when it is purchased.

Instead it is held on the balance sheet and its cost is depreciated over the years of its useful life.

In this case Oxfam has taken a more prudent approach and has charged the full cost of the assets in the income and expenditure account for the year of purchase.

(b) An asset should only be capitalised if future accounting periods will benefit from its use. This is not the case with vehicles and equipment used in operational programmes therefore their cost is charged in full as revenue expenditure in the year of purchase. (In fact, the information in Oxfam's accounting policy note states, 'The expected useful life of these assets is significantly reduced in such programmes').

6

Interpreting financial statements: Part 1

6.1 Introduction

In the next two chapters you will be learning how to analyse and interpret a set of financial statements. You will discover what questions you should ask about the accounts, and how and where to find the answers to these questions.

In this chapter you will be focusing on the profit and loss account and balance sheet, using them to assess the organisation's profitability, liquidity and efficiency. In Chapter 7 you will be looking at financial structure, and at how to assess a company's performance from the point of view of a shareholder or potential shareholder. In that chapter you will also be introduced to the analysis of cash flow statements.

6.2 Using ratios to analyse accounting statements

6.2.1 Why do we use ratios?

Let me tell you about my aunt Pamela. She owns a small newsagent's shop in our local town, employing one sales assistant, and seven school children who deliver morning papers. Suppose I told you that she earned £0.5 million profit from her business last year. Would you say that was a good result or a poor result?

Hopefully you would say that was a good result. It would be quite astonishing to earn an annual profit of £0.5 million from such a small, relatively low-risk enterprise!

Now consider a public limited company (plc) which owns a chain of newsagents, with an outlet in every high street and at every major railway station in the UK. If I told you that this plc earned £0.5 million profit last year, would you say that was a good result or a poor result?

This time you probably said that was a poor result. With so many outlets, you would expect a return of more than £0.5 million in one year.

The comparison of these two organisations is reasonably valid because they are in the same line of business.

If you agreed with my answers to these two questions, you were automatically relating the amount of profit to the size of the business earning the profit, i.e. you were performing a ratio analysis. A profit figure viewed in isolation is not very helpful in assessing an organisation's performance. However, if, for example, we relate the profit to the amount of money invested in the business (i.e. the size of the business) we can begin to judge whether or not the profit figure is adequate. Furthermore we can then legitimately compare the performance of two businesses.

A direct comparison of my aunt Pamela's profits with those of the large plc would obviously be unrealistic. We would expect that the plc's profits would be larger, but it would be difficult to state, in absolute terms, how much larger we expect them to be. However, if we express the profits in relation to some other figure, for example the business sales or the capital invested in the business, the resulting ratios would be comparable and would enable us to make some judgements about the businesses' performance.

6.2.2 Making comparisons

A ratio calculated in isolation is of little use unless there is some sort of yardstick or benchmark to compare it with. Suppose that the company you work for earned a return on the money invested in it (the capital employed) of 20 per cent last year. Would you say that was a good result or a poor result?

It is not possible for you to answer that question without making some sort of comparison. You probably answered 'it depends'. On what does it depend?

Exercise

Can you think of any bases that could be used to assess whether the 20 per cent return was a good result or a poor result?

Solution

You may have thought of the following bases:
- Compare with the same ratio for past periods. It may be possible to see whether there is a trend in the ratio over time.
- Compare with the budgeted or planned ratio for the period.
- Compare with the performance of other similar businesses.

6.2.3 The most common groups of ratios

There are dozens of ratios that could be used to analyse the performance of a business. In this book we will look at how to calculate and interpret the most common ratios.

The easiest way to approach a full ratio analysis is to group the ratios according to the particular aspect of business performance or financial position that they are attempting to monitor. We will consider five groups of ratios as follows.

- **Profitability**. Did the organisation make profitable use of the capital available to it? Was turnover adequate in relation to the amount of capital employed? Was the sales activity profitable?
- **Liquidity**. Can the company meet its current obligations as they fall due? How well equipped is it to pay its way in the short term?
- **Efficiency**. Is the business making efficient use of its resources?
- **Financial structure**. How much of the business's capital is contributed by the owners, and how much is contributed by outsiders?
- **Investment**. What returns are shareholders receiving on their investment? Is investor confidence in the company high or low?

The last two groups of ratios, financial structure and investment, will be reviewed in Chapter 7. In this chapter we will be discussing the assessment of profitability, liquidity and efficiency.

6.3 LMN plc's financial statements

The best way to demonstrate the interpretation of financial statements is to work through an example. Throughout this chapter and the next we will be referring to the following profit and loss accounts and balance sheets for LMN plc.

LMN plc: profit and loss accounts for the year ended 31 December

	Year 2 £m	Year 3 £m
Sales turnover	150.0	250
Cost of goods sold	100.0	175
Gross profit	50.0	75
Overhead costs	38.0	49
Operating profit	12.0	26
Interest	–	1
	12.0	25
Taxation	5.0	11
Net profit after taxation	7.0	14
Dividends	4.8	6
Retained profit to reserves	2.2	8

[handwritten annotations: "turnover – cost of goods sold", "cost of goods sold = op. profit + purch – closing TT", "paid out", "ready source of finance to help the w. grow."]

A reminder: operating profit is another term used to describe 'profit before interest and tax'.

LMN plc: balance sheet as at 31 December

	Year 2		Year 3	
	£m	£m	£m	£m
Fixed assets (net book value)		52.0		85
Current assets				
Stock	12.0		16	
Debtors	18.0		40	
Bank	10.0		4	
	40.0		60	
Current liabilities				
Creditors	10.2		28	
Dividends	4.8		6	
Taxation	5.0		11	
	20.0		45	
Net current assets		20.0		15
		72.0		100
Financed by:				
Ordinary £1 shares		60.0		60
Reserves – retained profit		12.0		20
Loan capital		–		20
		72.0		100

6.4 Begin with an overview

It is too easy to launch into calculating ratios without first stopping to look at the general trend in the organisation's performance and financial position: you should try to obtain a 'feel' for what has been happening. This will help you to interpret the ratios once they are calculated.

Exercise

Look at LMN plc's financial statements and write the answers to the following general questions.

- What is the movement in turnover?
- What is the movement in gross profit and in operating profit?
- Is the company investing in fixed assets?
- What is the movement in dividends?

Solution

LMN's activity has expanded dramatically. Turnover and profits have increased.

The company is investing in fixed assets. The balance sheet value of fixed assets has increased by more than 50 per cent, despite the depreciation charge for the year (you can also tell this by looking at the cash flow statement which is shown in Chapter 7).

Dividends have increased (look near the bottom of the profit and loss account). However, in year 3 they represented a smaller percentage of net profits. This means that the directors are retaining proportionately more of the profits to finance the company's growth.

6.5 Assessing profitability

The following ratios may be used to evaluate the organisation's profitability.

- Return on capital employed
- Net profit margin
- Asset turnover
- Gross profit margin

Strictly speaking, asset turnover is an efficiency ratio rather than a profitability ratio. However, it has been included here because, as you will see, it helps to explain the movement in the key profitability ratio: return on capital employed.

6.5.1 Return on capital employed (ROCE)

This is a fundamental ratio which is used to monitor business performance. It measures the amount of profit earned as a percentage of capital employed, i.e. it helps to provide the answer to the question that we were considering when evaluating the performance of my aunt Pamela's newsagent's shop: 'Is the profit sufficient considering the amount of capital invested to earn that profit?'

The return on capital employed (ROCE) is calculated as follows:.

$$\text{ROCE} = \frac{\text{Profit before interest and taxation}}{\text{Share capital + reserves + long-term loans}} \times 100\%$$

The profit figure is usually taken before interest because this is the profit that has been earned to pay all the providers of finance, i.e. the profit on the top of the calculation 'belongs' to the providers of finance on the bottom of the calculation.

Some analysts argue that profit before interest and tax (operating profit) is the most appropriate measure of an organisation's performance because it is the profit over which operational managers can exercise day-to-day control: they have some influence over this profit measure. If we chose profit after interest the performance would be distorted by the way in which the organisation is financed, i.e. by how much interest has to be paid. Operational managers have no direct influence over this. If we used net profit after taxation the performance would be distorted by the vagaries of the taxation charge, which again is outside the control of operational managers.

The ROCE for LMN for year 2 is:

$$\frac{12}{72} \times 100\% = 16.7\%$$

Exercise

Calculate LMN's ROCE for year 3.

Solution

$$\text{ROCE for year 3} = \frac{26}{100} \times 100\% = 26\%$$

The ROCE has improved dramatically. So now we need to start to look at why this has happened. We are going to perform a subanalysis of the ROCE, i.e. break it down into its constituent parts.

6.5.2 The constituent parts of ROCE

Returning for a moment to the example of a small newsagent's shop, suppose that you wanted to improve the shop's ROCE. What basic steps could you take to try and achieve an improvement?

Exercise

Name four basic steps that you could take to improve the ROCE of a newsagent's shop.

Solution

1. Put the prices up (assuming that this does not adversely affect sales)
2. Reduce costs
3. Sell more newspapers, etc.
4. Reduce the amount of capital employed

Steps 1 and 2 in the above solution can effectively be combined into one simple statement: 'earn more profit from each sale that is made.' This aspect of profitability is monitored by the net profit margin. This ratio relates the net profit to the sales value.

$$\text{Net profit margin} = \frac{\text{Profit before interest and taxation}}{\text{Sales turnover}} \times 100\%$$

Remember that we are trying to perform a subanalysis of the ROCE. Therefore we must use the same profit measure that we used in the ROCE calculation.

 The net profit margin may also be called the net profit percentage or the operating profit percentage.

Steps 3 and 4 could be stated in general terms as 'generate more sales per £1 of capital invested'.

This aspect of performance is measured by the asset turnover ratio, which monitors the level of sales relative to capital employed.

$$\text{Asset turnover} = \frac{\text{Sales turnover}}{\text{Share capital + reserves + long-term loans}}$$

Remember again that we are still performing a subanalysis of the ROCE. Therefore the figure for the capital employed (the denominator) must be the same as in the ROCE calculation.

Now we can put all this together to see the constituent parts of ROCE.

ROCE = net profit margin x asset turnover

$$\text{ROCE} = \frac{\text{Profit before interest and taxation}}{\text{Capital employed}}$$

$$= \frac{\text{Profit before interest and taxation}}{\text{Sales turnover}} \times \frac{\text{Sales turnover}}{\text{Capital employed}}$$

You should be able to see that when the formulae for net profit margin and asset turnover are multiplied together, the sales turnover on the top and bottom of the calculation cancels out, leaving the basic formula for the ROCE.

Therefore when we want to explore the reasons for changes in the ROCE, we can break it down between the profitability of sales (the net profit margin) and the level of sales achieved from the assets (the asset turnover).

Exercise

Use the data below to calculate the following ratios for year 4 for the two businesses:

- Return on capital employed (ROCE)
- Net profit margin
- Asset turnover

Year 4	The Posh Food Company £000	The Discount Food Company £000
Sales turnover	200	1,275
Operating profit	40	65
Capital employed	335	540

Solution

ROCE	$(^{40}/_{335})$ 11.9%	$(^{65}/_{540})$ 12.0%
Net profit margin	$(^{40}/_{200})$ 20.0%	$(^{65}/_{1,275})$ 5.1%
Asset turnover	$(^{200}/_{335})$ 0.6 times	$(^{1,275}/_{540})$ 2.4 times

For each company, you could check the following:
net profit margin x asset turnover = ROCE (approx.)

Notice that the asset turnover is usually expressed in terms of a number of times, rather than as a percentage.

It is worth looking in more detail at the results of this exercise. The ROCE is similar for both companies: about 12 per cent. Both companies are in the same business and therefore we might expect to see them earning the same sort of return for the same level of business risk.

However, you can see that each company has earned the overall ROCE in a quite different way. The Posh Food Company has earned a high margin on sales (20 per cent), possibly by charging higher prices, whereas The Discount Food Company has a comparatively low net profit margin (5.1 per cent) – their selling prices are probably relatively low. But The Discount Food Company has generated a much higher level of sales compared to capital employed (higher asset turnover) and this has compensated for the lower profit margin to produce a comparable overall ROCE.

You should now be in a position to analyse LMN's ROCE into its constituent parts.

6.5.3 Net profit margin for LMN

Exercise

Calculate LMN's net profit margin for years 2 and 3.

Solution

Net profit margin for year 2 = $\dfrac{12}{150}$ x 100% = 8.0%

Net profit margin for year 3 = $\dfrac{26}{250}$ x 100% = 10.4%

The net profit margin has improved in year 3 compared with year 2. This means that sales are being achieved more profitably. A smaller proportion of the sales value is being absorbed as costs. This has been a contributory factor in the improvement in ROCE.

6.5.4 Asset turnover for LMN

Exercise

Calculate LMN's asset turnover for years 2 and 3.

Solution

Asset turnover for year 2 = $\dfrac{150}{72}$ = 2.1 times

Asset turnover for year 3 = $\dfrac{250}{100}$ = 2.5 times

Sales achieved during year 2 were 2.1 times the level of capital employed. This is a measure of how efficiently the assets of the business were being used to generate sales. Generally, the higher the asset turnover, the more productively the assets were being used.

The asset turnover has improved in year 3 compared with year 2. This means that LMN's assets are being used more productively in year 3. More sales are being generated per £1 of capital invested in the assets. This has also been a contributory factor in the improvement in LMN's ROCE.

6.5.5 Gross profit margin

The gross profit margin relates the gross profit to the sales revenue for the period:

Gross profit margin = $\dfrac{\text{Gross profit}}{\text{Sales turnover}}$ x 100%

Look back to Chapter 2 if you have forgotten the difference between gross and net profit.

For many retailing and manufacturing organisations, the cost of the goods sold is a major part of total cost. Therefore this ratio can be of vital importance to the overall performance of this type of business.

$$\text{Gross profit margin for year 2} = \frac{50}{150} \times 100\% = 33.3\%$$

Exercise

Calculate LMN's gross profit margin for year 3.

Solution

$$\text{Gross profit margin for year 3} = \frac{75}{250} \times 100\% = 30\%$$

6.5.6 LMN's profitability ratios: summary

The ratios that we have calculated for years 2 and 3 are as follows.

	Year 2	Year 3
Return on capital employed	16.7%	26.0%
Net profit margin	8.0%	10.4%
Asset turnover	2.1 times	2.5 times
Gross profit margin	33.3%	30.0%

Exercise

What general conclusions can you draw about LMN's profitability during year 3?

Solution

ROCE has improved dramatically, due to increases in both the asset turnover and the net profit margin, i.e. not only is more being sold in year 3, but it is also being sold more profitably than in year 2.

The gross profit percentage has decreased. This could be due to an increase in the cost of goods sold. However, it is more likely that the selling price of goods has been reduced in order to stimulate the increase in sales turnover. This has reduced the gross profitability of sales, but the extra volume has helped to make sales more profitable at the operating profit level.

Later in this text you will learn that part of the reason for this increase in profitability is the spreading of fixed costs (i.e. costs that do not increase with sales) over a higher level of sales.

6.5.7 Problems with the use and interpretation of ROCE

A number of problems arise with the use and interpretation of ROCE:

(a) The main problem with ROCE is that the definition of capital employed can vary, as can the profit figure used for the numerator. Different analysts will calculate the ratio in different ways, therefore care is needed when comparing two calculated ROCEs. It is essential to ensure that they are both calculated using the same method.

(b) ROCE can give a misleading guide to efficiency if a company's assets are not valued at current prices, for example if a company's land and buildings have increased in value but this increase is not reflected on the balance sheet.

(c) Linked to problem (b), capital investment often results in low returns in the early years and an annual calculation of ROCE may therefore be distorted in the short term by investment in longer-term projects. The following example will help to illustrate this point.

Example

A company is about to invest in a new machine. This will cost £1,000 and will last for five years, after which time it will have no value. During its five-year life the machine will generate an annual profit of £100, after taking account of depreciation.

The return on the capital employed in this machine for each of the five years could be calculated as follows.

End of year		Net book value of machine		ROCE
		£		%
1	(£1,000 – £200)	800	$(^{100}/_{800})$	12.5
2	(£800 – £200)	600	$(^{100}/_{600})$	16.7
3	(£600 – £200)	400	$(^{100}/_{400})$	25.0
4	(£400 – £200)	200	$(^{100}/_{200})$	50.0
5	(£200 – £200)	0	$(^{100}/_{0})$	infinite

 The annual depreciation charge is (£1,000 ÷ 5 =) £200. This is the amount by which the net book value is reduced each year.

This simple example demonstrates that the lower the net book value of the asset, the higher will be the ROCE for a given level of profit. Therefore new capital investment can depress the ROCE in the short term, and if assets are undervalued then the ROCE may be misleadingly high.

6.6 Assessing liquidity

The liquidity of an organisation refers to its ability to meet its current liabilities as they fall due. A bank manager might be interested in an organisation's liquidity if they have requested overdraft facilities. Or perhaps a company has been approached by a new customer who requires credit for all supplies. The supplying company may first review the customer's liquidity position before deciding to grant credit facilities.

The following ratios may be used to evaluate the organisation's liquidity:

- Current ratio
- Acid test ratio (also called the quick ratio or the liquid ratio)

6.6.1 Current ratio

This ratio relates an organisation's current assets to its current liabilities to assess its ability to meet its short-term obligations and is calculated as follows:

$$\text{Current ratio} = \frac{\text{Current assets}}{\text{Current liabilities}}$$

The current ratio for LMN for year 2 is:

$$\frac{40}{20} = 2 \text{ times}$$

This means that the current assets cover the current liabilities twice at the end of year 2.

Exercise

Calculate LMN's current ratio for year 3.

Solution

$$\text{Current ratio} = \frac{60}{45} = 1.3 \text{ times}$$

The current assets covered the current liabilities 1.3 times at the end of year 3.

6.6.2 Is there an 'ideal' size for the current ratio?

The 'ideal' size for the current ratio depends on a number of factors, including the following:

- **The past record for the company**. It is preferable to look at the trend in the current ratio over a number of years. Generally, the higher the current ratio, the more liquid the organisation. Since liquidity is important to the organisation's survival it may be a cause for concern if the current ratio is reducing. If the current ratio falls too low the organisation may be in danger of overtrading. This happens when the organisation enters into commitments which are in excess of its available short-term resources. However, if the current ratio is too high, funds may be unnecessarily tied up in stocks or debtors that could be used more efficiently elsewhere in the organisation.

- **The type of business and the 'norm' for the industry**. For example a retailing company might be expected to have a lower current ratio than a manufacturing company. In fact, many retailing companies have a current ratio of less than 1.0, indicating that the current liabilities exceed the current assets, i.e. these companies have net current liabilities or negative working capital.

Exercise

Explain why retailing companies tend to have a lower current ratio than manufacturing companies.

Solution

The current asset balances of retailing companies tend to be relatively lower than the current asset balances of manufacturing companies for the following reasons:

- Retailing companies do not hold stocks of raw materials or work in progress. Furthermore, their finished goods stocks are likely to be low in value compared with the finished goods stocks of a manufacturing company.
- Retailing companies sell mostly on a cash basis and so have very few debtors on their balance sheet. Manufacturing companies may have to wait for several weeks before cash payment is received from their debtors.

6.6.3 The acid test ratio

This ratio may also be called the quick ratio or the liquid ratio. It is used to give a more stringent assessment of an organisation's liquidity.

In many organisations it may take quite a long time to convert stocks into cash. For example, the manufacturing process may be such that it takes several days or even weeks to produce a finished product, and on top of this customers may expect a lengthy period of credit. Therefore it could be argued that in this type of organisation stocks are not a liquid asset: they cannot be quickly liquidated to meet current liabilities as they become due. The 'acid test' of an organisation's liquidity is whether it can cover its current liabilities without having to sell its stocks, i.e. this ratio includes only the liquid assets in the calculation:

$$\text{Acid test ratio} = \frac{\text{Current assets } \textit{excluding} \text{ stock}}{\text{Current liabilities}}$$

Exercise

Calculate LMN's acid test ratio for years 2 and 3.

Solution

$$\text{Year 2} = \frac{28}{20} = 1.4 \text{ times} \qquad \text{Year 3} = \frac{44}{45} = 0.98 \text{ times}$$

In year 2, LMN's liquid assets covered its current liabilities 1.4 times. However, in year 3 the ratio has fallen below 1.0 therefore LMN would have to sell some of the stock to meet all its current liabilities.

6.6.4 Using balance sheet information

It is important to appreciate that the liquidity ratios that we have calculated in this section are based on balance sheet data. The balance sheet is like a photograph taken of the organisation at the end of the financial year. Therefore the working capital balances may not be representative of the liquidity position during the year. There may have been exceptional events at the end of the year or the business may be seasonal, leading to higher or lower than average working capital balances at the end of the year.

6.6.5 LMN's liquidity ratios: summary

The ratios that we have calculated for years 2 and 3 are as follows.

	Year 2	Year 3
Current ratio	2 times	1.3 times
Acid test ratio	1.4 times	0.98 times

Exercise

What outline conclusions can you draw about LMN's short-term liquidity position at the end of year 3?

Solution

We do not know what business LMN is in, therefore we cannot comment on what would be a suitable current ratio. However, the change in the two liquidity ratios may be a cause for concern. They have both deteriorated and in year 3 it is not possible for LMN to meet its current liabilities without having to sell some stock. The year 3 ratios in themselves are not necessarily too low and it is difficult to draw firm conclusions without knowing the sort of business that LMN is in. However, the change from year 2 levels could indicate liquidity problems if it is not a controlled change. The company appears to be in danger of overtrading.

6.7 Assessing efficiency

This group of ratios assesses whether the organisation is making efficient use of its resources. Ratios that may be calculated under this category include the following:

- Stock turnover period
- Debtors collection period
- Creditors payment period

6.7.1 Stock turnover period

This ratio measures the average number of days' stock held on the balance sheet date. It can be calculated for LMN in year 2 as follows:

$$\text{Stock turnover period} = \frac{\text{Stock}}{\text{Cost of sales per day}} = \frac{12}{(^{100}/_{365})} = 44 \text{ days}$$

This means that, based on the average cost of sales per day during year 2, the year-end stocks represented 44 days' worth of sales. However, as with the liquidity ratios, it is important to bear in mind that this ratio is based on year-end balance sheet data. The stockholdings may not be representative of what has been held during the year.

Exercise

Calculate LMN's stock turnover period for year 3.

Solution

$$\text{Stock turnover for year 3} = \frac{16}{^{175}/_{365}} = 33 \text{ days}$$

Generally a low stock turnover period is preferable, i.e. stock should be held for the shortest time possible. The ability to manage a business on very low stocks depends, among other things, on the quality of the management information systems and on the closeness of relationships with suppliers, and their reliability.

Exercise

Can you think of reasons why stock should be held for the shortest time possible? And can you think of when this policy might lead to problems?

Solution

Your reasons for a short stockholding period may have included the following:

- Capital tied up in stock could be used more effectively elsewhere.
- The longer stock is held, the more likely it is to become unusable or obsolete. This is particularly important with perishable items or fashion goods.
- Higher stocks will generally incur higher storage costs, higher insurance costs, etc.

If stocks are too low this could lead to the following problems:

- Stocks may run out, leading to lost opportunities or the need to make emergency purchases at higher prices.
- If goods are purchased in small quantities, bulk discounts may be forgone and ordering costs may be high.

6.7.2 Debtors collection period

The debtors collection period measures how long, on average, credit customers take to settle their bill and is calculated as follows:

$$\text{Debtors collection period} = \frac{\text{Trade debtors}}{\text{Credit sales per day}}$$

Exercise

Assuming that all LMN's sales are made on credit, calculate the debtors collection period for years 2 and 3.

Solution

$$\text{Year 2} = \frac{18}{\left(^{150}/_{365}\right)} = 44 \text{ days} \qquad \text{Year 3} = \frac{40}{\left(^{250}/_{365}\right)} = 58 \text{ days}$$

On average, it took longer to collect debts from customers in year 3 than in year 2. This can have a detrimental effect on the cash flows and liquidity of the company. Furthermore, the longer a debtor takes to pay, the higher the risk that the debtor will run into financial difficulties and be unable to pay.

Once again it is important to bear in mind the inadequacies of the balance sheet figure in calculating the number of days' debt. The resulting figure is an average which may not be representative of the year as a whole, and it might be distorted by the existence of, say, one large customer who is exceptionally slow to pay.

6.7.3 Creditors payment period

The debtors collection period could be compared with the creditors payment period:

$$\text{Creditors payment period} = \frac{\text{Trade creditors}}{\text{Credit purchases per day}}$$

Management sometimes try to ensure that the two periods are roughly equal, or that the creditors period is slightly longer, i.e. that the organisation takes longer to pay its bills than it takes to collect money from its customers, resulting in interest-free credit for a period.

However, this policy should not be pursued to extremes. The organisation may gain a reputation for being a slow payer resulting in higher prices, or the supplier might even curtail supplies.

The data that we have for LMN does not show the purchases made each year. This is often the case with published accounts and it is commonly accepted that a reasonable approximation is to use instead the figures for cost of goods sold.

Exercise

Using cost of goods sold instead of purchases in the above formula, calculate the average creditors payment period for LMN in years 2 and 3.

Solution

$$\text{Year 2} = \frac{10.2}{\left(^{100}\!/_{365}\right)} = 37 \text{ days} \qquad \text{Year 3} = \frac{28}{\left(^{175}\!/_{365}\right)} = 58 \text{ days}$$

The average creditors payment period has shown a substantial increase. In year 3, LMN took, on average, nearly two months to pay for its purchases. Remember that the use of balance sheet data presents the same interpretation problems with this ratio as with the debtors collection period.

6.7.4 LMN's efficiency ratios: summary

The ratios that we have calculated for years 2 and 3 are as follows.

	Year 2	Year 3
Stock turnover period	44 days	33 days
Debtors collection period	44 days	58 days
Creditors payment period	37 days	58 days

Exercise

What outline conclusions can you draw about LMN's management of its working capital resources in years 2 and 3?

Solution

Debtor levels appear to be increasing out of control, although this may be a deliberate and controlled increase as part of a policy to encourage increased sales.

Stock levels appear to have reduced. This indicates efficient control of working capital, although sales may be lost if customer requirements cannot be met from stock.

Creditor levels have been reasonably well matched with debtors. However, supplier relationships may be harmed if the credit period becomes excessive.

6.8 Summary

1. Ratios are widely used in the analysis of financial statements. They enable one figure to be related to another and facilitate comparison between organisations of different size.

2. The following five groups of ratios may be used to analyse a set of financial statements:
   - Profitability
   - Liquidity
   - Efficiency
   - Financial structure
   - Investment

3. Before beginning on a ratio analysis it is important to look at the financial statements to obtain an overall 'feel' for what has been happening during the period covered by the statements.

Review questions

1. How is the return on capital employed (ROCE) calculated? (section 6.5.1)
2. If there has been a change in the ROCE which is worth further investigation, which two ratios can be used to subanalyse the ROCE? (section 6.5.2)
3. If a company's assets are undervalued, will ROCE tend to be under- or overstated? (section 6.5.7)
4. What is the difference between the two main ratios used to assess liquidity: the current ratio and the acid test ratio? (sections 6.6.1, 6.6.3)
5. How is the stock turnover period calculated and what is the significance of a relatively long stock turnover period? (section 6.7.1)

Self-test questions

1. Other things being equal, would the following events, each considered separately, cause the return on capital employed to increase or decrease?

   (a) Increase in stock
   (b) Decrease in asset turnover
   (c) Decrease in debtors
   (d) Increase in net profit margin
   (e) Increase in creditors

2. RC Ltd manufactures and sells non-perishable food products to the retail trade. A summary of the latest profit and loss accounts and balance sheets is as follows.

   RC Ltd: profit and loss accounts for the year ended 31 March

	Year 7 £000	Year 8 £000
Sales	183	170
Less cost of sales	71	55
Gross margin	112	115
Overhead expenses	76	78
Operating profit before interest and tax	36	37
Interest	4	6
	32	31
Taxation	8	7
Net profit after taxation	24	24
Dividend proposed	15	10
Retained profit to reserves	9	14

RC Ltd: balance sheets as at 31 March

	Year 7		Year 8	
	£000	£000	£000	£000
Fixed assets (net book value)		94		130
Current assets				
Stock	8		5	
Debtors	22		15	
Bank	16		12	
	46		32	
Current liabilities				
Trade creditors	8		8	
Other creditors and accruals	3		2	
Dividends	15		10	
Taxation	8		7	
	34		27	
Net current assets		12		5
		106		135
Creditors: amounts due after more than one year				
Bank loans		25		40
		81		95
Ordinary £1 shares		50		50
Reserves – retained profit		31		45
		81		95

Required:
Prepare an analysis of RC Ltd's profitability, liquidity and efficiency of working capital management for years 7 and 8.

Answers to self-test questions

1. (a) An increase in stock would cause the return on capital employed (ROCE) to decrease, because the amount of capital employed (the denominator in the ROCE calculation) would increase.

   (b) A decrease in asset turnover would tend to cause the ROCE to decrease because lower sales are being achieved for a given level of capital employed.

   (c) A decrease in debtors would cause the ROCE to increase, because the amount of capital employed (the denominator in the ROCE calculation) would decrease.

   (d) An increase in net profit margin would cause the ROCE to increase.

The net profit margin and the asset turnover can be multiplied together to determine the ROCE. Other things being equal, if the net profit margin increases then so will the ROCE.

(e) An increase in creditors would cause the ROCE to increase, because the amount of capital employed (the denominator in the ROCE calculation) would decrease.

2. The first thing to notice is that RC Ltd's balance sheet is arranged slightly differently. The long term bank loans are shown as a deduction from the 'assets side' of the balance sheet. This is a common form of presentation. It does not affect the analysis, but it does mean that a little more care is needed in determining the correct figure for capital employed.

Profitability

$$\text{ROCE} = \frac{\text{profit before interest and taxation}}{\text{share capital + reserves + long-term loans}} \times 100\% = 33.3\%$$

Year 7 *Year 8*

$$\text{ROCE} = \frac{36}{106} \times 100\% = 34.0\% \qquad \frac{37}{135} \times 100\% = 27.4\%$$

$$\text{Net profit margin} = \frac{\text{profit before interest and taxation}}{\text{sales}} \times 100\%$$

Year 7 *Year 8*

$$\text{Net profit margin} = \frac{36}{183} \times 100\% = 19.7\% \qquad \frac{37}{170} \times 100\% = 21.8\%$$

$$\text{Asset turnover} = \frac{\text{sales}}{\text{share capital + reserves + long-term loans}}$$

Year 7 *Year 8*

$$\text{Asset turnover} = \frac{183}{106} = 1.7 \text{ times} \qquad \frac{170}{135} = 1.3 \text{ times}$$

$$\text{Gross profit margin} = \frac{\text{gross profit}}{\text{sales}} \times 100\%$$

	Year 7	Year 8

Gross profit margin = $\dfrac{112}{183}$ x 100% = 61.2% $\dfrac{115}{170}$ x 100% = 67.6%

RC Limited's return on capital employed deteriorated in year 8, due to a reduction in the asset turnover. A lower level of sales was combined with an increase in the capital employed (there was a substantial increase in the level of fixed asset investment).

The profitability of sales, at the net profit level and at the gross profit level, improved and this lessened the impact of the reduced asset turnover.

Liquidity

		Year 7	Year 8

Current ratio = $\dfrac{\text{current assets}}{\text{current liabilities}}$ $\dfrac{46}{34}$ = 1.4 times $\dfrac{32}{27}$ = 1.2 times

Acid test ratio = $\dfrac{\text{current assets - stock}}{\text{current liabilities}}$ $\dfrac{38}{34}$ = 1.1 times $\dfrac{27}{27}$ = 1.0 times

RC Limited's liquidity has deteriorated slightly but the current assets are sufficient to cover the current liabilities in year 8, even without the stock.

Efficiency of working capital management

		Year 7	Year 8

Stock turnover period = $\dfrac{\text{stock}}{\text{cost of sales per day}}$ $\dfrac{8}{^{71}/_{365}}$ = 41 days $\dfrac{5}{^{55}/_{365}}$ = 33 days

Debtors collection period = $\dfrac{\text{debtors}}{\text{sales per day}}$ $\dfrac{22}{^{183}/_{365}}$ = 44 days $\dfrac{15}{^{170}/_{365}}$ = 32 days

Creditor payment period = $\dfrac{\text{trade creditors}}{\text{cost of sales per day}}$ $\dfrac{8}{^{71}/_{365}}$ = 41 days $\dfrac{8}{^{55}/_{365}}$ = 53 days

The average stockholding period has reduced by eight days, which is an improvement as long as customer service is maintained.

The average debtor collection period has reduced by twelve days. This demonstrates improved working capital control, but could it have contributed to the reduction in sales turnover, due to customers going elsewhere to receive better credit terms?

The average creditor payment period has increased by twelve days. This probably demonstrates improved working capital control, as long as it is not leading to higher purchase prices or loss of supplier goodwill.

7

Interpreting financial statements: Part 2

7.1 Introduction

In this chapter you will be learning more about how to interpret financial statements. We will be continuing our review of LMN plc, looking first at the company's financial structure and then at its performance from the point of view of shareholders and potential shareholders. We will also be interpreting the cash-flow statement.

7.2 Financial structure

There are two important ratios which help in analysing a company's financial structure.

- The gearing ratio
- The interest cover ratio

7.2.1 What is financial gearing?

Gearing refers to the proportion of a company's funds that are provided by debt on which fixed interest is payable.

If a company has a large amount of loan capital compared to shareholders' funds, it is said to be high geared.

If a company has a small amount of loan capital compared to shareholders' funds, it is said to be low geared.

Gearing has important implications for management because if the company is high geared it means that managers must react quickly if sales start to fall. Shareholders will also be interested in the level of gearing, because any changes in sales could have a dramatic effect on their fortunes if the company is high geared.

The following example will demonstrate why this happens.

Example: the effect of financial gearing

Two companies, High Gear Limited and Low Gear Limited, each have the same amount of capital in total, but different proportions of share capital and loan capital as follows:

	High Gear Limited £	Low Gear Limited £
Share capital: £1 shares	100,000	250,000
Loan capital	200,000	50,000
	300,000	300,000

The annual interest rate on the loan capital is 10 per cent.

 Notice that two-thirds of High Gear's capital comes from loans, whereas only one-sixth of Low Gear's capital consists of loans.

Suppose that the profit for the year, before interest, amounts to £30,000 for each company. The profit per share (ignoring taxation) can be calculated as follows:

	£000		£000
Profit before interest	30		30
Interest (200,000 x 10%)	20	(50,000 x 10%)	5
Profit after interest	10		25

Profit per share (ignoring tax)	($^{10}/_{100}$) £0.10	($^{25}/_{250}$) £0.10

At this level of profits there is no difference in the fortunes of the shareholders.

Now let us see what happens if the profit before interest doubles to £60,000.

	£000		£000
Profit before interest	60		60
Interest (200,000 x 10%)	20	(50,000 x 10%)	5
Profit after interest	40		55

Profit per share (ignoring tax)	($^{40}/_{100}$) £0.40	($^{55}/_{250}$) £0.22

The profit per share has more than doubled for both companies, since both have some gearing. However, the change in profit is magnified dramatically for the high geared company, therefore the returns for shareholders increase considerably.

On the other hand, if profits begin to fall then the profit per share will reduce faster with the high geared company than with the lower-geared one.

Exercise

In the above example of High Gear Limited and Low Gear Limited, calculate the profit per share for each company if annual profits before interest fall to £24,000.

Solution

	High Gear Limited	Low Gear Limited
	£000	£000
Profit before interest	24	24
Interest (200,000 x 10%)	20	(50,000 x 10%) 5
Profit after interest	4	19
Profit per share (ignoring tax)	($^4/_{100}$) £0.04	($^{19}/_{250}$) £0.08

The fall in profits has caused a greater reduction in the profit per share for the highly geared company.

The managers of a highly geared company must therefore be careful to maintain the level of profits and sales and must react quickly if sales or profits start to fall. However, if sales and profits increase, the shareholders in a highly geared company will be proportionately much better off.

This volatility of returns which is caused by the existence of higher levels of gearing reflects the financial risk associated with high gearing.

7.2.2 Is there an ideal level of gearing?

The most appropriate level of gearing will depend on the type of business that the company is in. Different types of business bring with them different levels of business risk. Business risk is assessed by the potential variability in a company's profits from one year to the next.

Exercise

Which would you say has the higher level of business risk: a company which manufactures luxury fashion goods or a company which manufactures bread?

Solution

The fashion goods company would be exposed to greater business risk than would a company which manufactures bread, because the potential variability in profits is higher.

Demand for the fashion goods is likely to be more volatile than the demand for bread. The demand for fashion goods would depend on changes in fashion, on the activities of competitors, and on the amount of money that consumers have to spend.

Demand for bread would probably be more stable, hence this company would experience smaller fluctuations in profit and therefore a lower level of business risk.

We have seen that high gearing leads to high financial risk because of the potentially exaggerated fluctuations in the returns to shareholders. The total risk of a company is made up of its financial risk and business risk. Potential investors and lenders will assess the total level of risk in a company. Generally, for a given level of desired total risk, the higher a company's business risk, the lower its financial risk should be, i.e. the lower its desirable level of gearing.

7.2.3 Calculating the gearing ratio

There are many different methods that might be used to calculate the gearing ratio. The most important thing is to be consistent and to ensure, if you are comparing gearing ratios, that they have been calculated using the same method.

In this text the following formula will be used:

$$\text{Gearing ratio} = \frac{\text{Fixed interest loans} + \text{preference share capital}}{\text{Total capital employed}} \times 100\%$$

Overdrafts are usually included as part of fixed-interest loans, despite the fact that they are not really part of long-term capital.

Preference share capital is usually included with the fixed interest capital. You should recall that a preference share is a special type of share which is entitled to a fixed rate of return each year.

In contrast to lenders, preference shareholders cannot force the company to pay them their fixed annual return. However, in practical terms the company must pay the preference dividend in order to maintain investor confidence in the company.

In our example, LMN's gearing ratio for year 2 is zero, since it has no borrowing and no preference shares.

Exercise

Calculate LMN's gearing ratio for year 3.

Solution

$$\text{Gearing, year 3} = \frac{20}{100} \times 100\% = 20\%$$

LMN's gearing ratio has increased due to the introduction of loan capital during year 3. This has increased the financial risk associated with LMN.

We do not know what type of business LMN is engaged in, therefore it is difficult to comment on whether this is an acceptable level of financial risk commensurate with LMN's business risk. Certainly the change may cause alarm to some investors but, on the other hand, they may welcome the potentially higher returns that accompany the introduction of a modest level of gearing.

7.2.4 Interest cover

This ratio monitors the amount of profit that was available to cover the interest payment for the year. The higher the cover, the more able the business was to meet its fixed interest commitments.

$$\text{Interest cover} = \frac{\text{Profit before interest and tax}}{\text{Interest payable}}$$

Exercise

Calculate LMN's interest cover ratio for year 3 and comment on the result.

Solution

$$\text{Interest cover, year 3} = \frac{26}{1} = 26 \text{ times}$$

This is a very high interest cover: it appears that LMN could have paid the interest 26 times over (but see the next paragraph!).

The result of this exercise could be misleading. It is important to bear in mind that the loan was probably not held for the whole of the year (this is the problem with placing too much weight on balance sheet figures). Therefore, the interest for a full year is likely to be more than £1 million and the interest cover is in reality lower than 26 times.

However, even if the interest rate was as high as 25 per cent, the annual interest on the loan would be only £5 million (£20 million x 25 per cent). In that case the interest cover would be 5.2 times (£26m/£5m).

As with the gearing ratio, the desirable level of interest cover will depend on the company's business risk.

7.3 Investment ratios

The following ratios can be used to assess the company's performance from the point of view of a shareholder or potential shareholder:

- Return on shareholders' funds (also called the return on shareholders' equity)
- Ordinary dividend cover
- Dividend yield
- Earnings yield
- Earnings per share
- Price–earnings ratio

7.3.1 Return on shareholders' funds

This is very similar to ROCE, except that it focuses on the returns to ordinary shareholders. Remember that ordinary shares entitle the holders to the profits that remain after everybody else has received their entitlement, e.g. after tax, interest and preference dividend has been paid. They literally are 'at the bottom of the pile', in distribution of profits as well as in repayment of capital in a liquidation.

Ordinary shareholders tend to do well when business fortunes are good, because everybody else receives only their fixed return and all other returns belong to the ordinary shareholders (see our earlier discussion on gearing). On the other hand, they have no recourse if business is not going so well. They are really the 'risk-taking' investors in the business.

 The level of risk taken by ordinary shareholders in any particular company will depend on the company's total risk, i.e. on the combination of its business risk and its financial risk.

The return on shareholders' funds (ROSF) is calculated as follows:

$$\text{ROSF} = \frac{\text{Profits after interest, tax and preference dividends}}{\text{Ordinary share capital + reserves}} \times 100\%$$

You may recall that the ordinary shareholders' investment in the business, in terms of share capital plus reserves, is sometimes called the equity. For this reason the ratio is sometimes called the return on equity.

Exercise

Calculate LMN's return on shareholders' funds for years 2 and 3.

Solution

	Year 2	Year 3
Return on shareholders' funds		
$(^{7}/_{72} \times 100\%)$	9.7%	
$(^{14}/_{80} \times 100\%)$		17.5%

7.3.2 Ordinary dividend cover

This is similar to the interest cover ratio. It measures how 'safe' the dividend payment was, i.e. how many times the current year's profit could have covered the dividend payout. If the dividend cover falls to very low levels, shareholders may not be able to rely on the current level of dividends being maintained in the future.

$$\text{Ord. div. cover} = \frac{\text{Profits after interest, tax and pref. dividends}}{\text{Ordinary dividend for the year}}$$

LMN does not have any preference shares, therefore all of the dividend is ordinary dividend.

If the ordinary dividend cover is consistently low, it indicates that the directors have a general policy of paying out a large proportion of the year's profits as dividends, i.e. they do not plough back a large proportion of the profits as a source of finance for the company.

Exercise

Calculate LMN's ordinary dividend cover in years 2 and 3.

Solution

	Year 2	Year 3
Ordinary dividend cover		
$(^{7.0}/_{4.8})$	1.5 times	
$(^{14}/_{6})$		2.3 times

7.3.3 Dividend yield

This is a market-related ratio which cannot be calculated based only on the information contained within a set of published accounts. A further piece of information is needed: the share's current market price. In the case of our LMN example, let us assume that the share price at 31 December of each year was as follows:

Year 2	Year 3
£1.44	£2.30

This is additional information which would not usually be available in published accounts.

The dividend yield assesses the cash return to shareholders compared with the amount of money they have invested to earn that cash return.

$$\text{Dividend yield} = \frac{\text{Dividend per share}}{\text{Market price of share}} \times 100\%$$

Exercise

Calculate LMN's shareholders' dividend yield for years 2 and 3.

Solution

	Year 2	Year 3
Dividend yield		
$[(^{4.8}/_{60}) \div 1.44] \times 100\%$	5.6%	
$[(^{6.0}/_{60}) \div 2.30] \times 100\%$		4.3%

However, the dividend is only a part of the return earned for the ordinary shareholders. The part of the profits that was taken to reserves has also been earned for them, even if they have not received it from the company in the form of a cash return. It has been invested in the company on their behalf in order to earn them a capital gain.

Therefore to gain a full assessment of the returns earned for the ordinary shareholders, the **earnings** must be taken into account.

Earnings is a term used to describe the profits earned for the ordinary shareholders during the year. It is the profit after deduction of interest, tax and preference dividend, i.e. after all other interested parties have been allocated their share of the profits.

7.3.4 Earnings yield

This ratio assesses the total percentage return that shareholders have received on their investment, regardless of whether it was actually paid to shareholders in cash. Part of the earnings may have been paid out as dividend, the remainder has been kept in the business for reinvestment.

$$\text{Earnings yield} = \frac{\text{Current-year profit attributable to each ord. share}}{\text{Market price of share}} \times 100\%$$

 Earnings yield is another ratio that cannot be calculated based on published accounts. The market price of the share is needed.

 Exercise
Calculate LMN's earnings yield for years 2 and 3.

 Solution

	Year 2	Year 3
Earnings yield		
$[(^7/_{60}) \div 1.44] \times 100\%$	8.1%	
$[(^{14}/_{60}) \div 2.30] \times 100\%$		10.1%

7.3.5 Earnings per share (EPS)

This ratio relates the earnings for the year to the number of shares in issue. Many analysts regard this as a fundamental measure of a company's performance, and the trend of the EPS over time can be particularly important.

$$\text{EPS} = \frac{\text{Current-year profit attributable to ord. shareholders}}{\text{Number of ordinary shares}} \times 100\%$$

 'Current year's profit attributable to ordinary shareholders' is the same as 'profit after deduction of interest, tax and preference dividend', which is the same as 'earnings'. Remember that we are simply describing the ordinary shareholders' return after everybody else has received their allocation. Unfortunately, in practice you will come across all these different descriptions of the same item.

 Exercise
Calculate LMN's EPS for years 2 and 3.

 Solution

	Year 2	Year 3
Earnings per share		
$(^7/_{60})$	11.7 pence	
$(^{14}/_{60})$		23.3 pence

7.3.6 Price–earnings (PE) ratio

This ratio relates the market price of a share to its annual earnings. It represents the number of times the annual earnings for each share that investors are willing to pay to acquire a share.

$$\text{Price–earnings ratio} = \frac{\text{Market price of share}}{\text{Earnings per share}}$$

Exercise

Calculate LMN's PE ratio based on the earnings for years 2 and 3.

Solution

	Year 2	Year 3
Price–earnings ratio		
$(1.44/0.117)$	12.3 times	
$(2.30/0.233)$		9.9 times

A high PE ratio indicates that investors have high confidence in the future prospects for a company. However, it is important to compare companies which are in the same type of business, as average PE ratios will vary from industry to industry.

7.3.7 LMN's investment ratios: summary

	Year 2	Year 3
Return on shareholders' funds	9.7%	17.5%
Ordinary dividend cover	1.5 times	2.3 times
Dividend yield	5.6%	4.3%
Earnings yield	8.1%	10.1%
Earnings per share	11.7 pence	23.3 pence
Price–earnings ratio	12.3 times	9.9 times

Exercise

Comment on LMN's performance from the point of view of a shareholder or potential shareholder.

Solution

The return on shareholders' funds has improved during year 3, in line with the overall improvement in LMN's fortunes. The adequacy of this return will depend on the shareholders' attitude to risk (the financial risk has increased with the level of gearing) and on the other opportunities that shareholders have for the investment of their funds.

The level of dividend cover has improved, but this also indicates that directors are retaining proportionately more of the annual earnings for reinvestment. The importance of this will depend on shareholders' need for cash returns versus capital gains.

Dividend yield has deteriorated because although the absolute amount of dividend has increased, the dividend per share has not increased at the same rate as the share's market price.

The earnings yield and the earnings per share have increased. Shareholders are achieving a higher return on their investment in LMN's shares. As above, the adequacy of these ratios will depend on the shareholders' attitude to risk and on the other investment opportunities available.

The price–earnings ratio has deteriorated. Despite the increased earnings, the share price has not increased proportionately. This indicates a reduction in investors' assessment of the future prospects for this company. Perhaps they are not happy about the increase in gearing, or they may be disturbed by the deterioration in LMN's liquidity position.

7.4 Limitations of ratio analysis

Throughout this chapter and Chapter 6 you have seen warnings about the difficulties of making inter-company comparisons and drawing firm conclusions from an analysis based on published accounts. It will be useful to summarise in this section the main limitations of ratio analysis:

(a) Ratios are constructed from accounting data and they therefore inherit the subjective aspects of this data, e.g. differing depreciation policies may make it difficult to compare ratios from one company to another.
(b) If the accounts are made up to different dates, then different external factors may have influenced the figures, for example different trading conditions, which again makes comparison difficult.
(c) The results of ratios may be interpreted in different ways, for example a high stock turnover ratio may indicate efficient stock control or it may result from serious stock shortages.

(d) If only one or two years' figures are available then there is no reference to trends over recent years.

(e) There is no reference to future prospects or plans (although the PE ratio may take account of shareholders' view of the company's future prospects).

(f) The focus tends to be on relative rather than absolute values, for example some profitability ratios can look good if the assets are undervalued (this can result in a smaller denominator).

(g) The ratios are based on balance sheet data, which may not be representative of the year as a whole.

7.5 Interpreting cash-flow statements

To complete our analysis of LMN's performance and financial position we will now look at the following cash-flow statements for years 2 and 3.

LMN plc: cash-flow statement for the year ended 31 December

	Year 2	Year 3
	£m	£m
Net cash inflow from operating activities	14.2	21.3
Returns on investments and		
servicing of finance	–	(0.7)
Corporation tax paid	(3.7)	(5.0)
Capital expenditure	(6.2)	(36.8)
	4.3	(21.2)
Equity dividends paid	(3.2)	(4.8)
	1.1	(26.0)
Financing	–	20.0
Increase/(decrease) in cash	1.1	(6.0)

The interpretation of cash flows is fraught with difficulties because cash flows are so volatile. For this reason it is important not to read too much into a single year's cash flows. However, a number of aspects of a cash-flow statement are worth investigating:

- The net cash flow from operating activities should be a positive figure. It should be sufficient to cover interest, tax and dividend payments and should make some contribution towards capital expenditure.

Exercise

Based on the above guideline, would you say that LMN's cash flows from operating activities in years 2 and 3 were adequate?

Solution

In year 2 the net cash inflow from operating activities was more than adequate to cover payments for dividends and tax, and to contribute towards the purchase of fixed assets.

In year 3 there was a positive cash inflow from operating activities which easily covered the payments for interest, dividend and tax. The contribution remaining towards capital expenditure amounted to £10.8 million (£21.3m – £0.7m – £5.0m – £4.8m) but this did not cover the full amount of the investment in fixed assets. However, the cash flow from operating activities was probably adequate, since the investment in fixed assets during year 3 was relatively large.

- If there is a net outflow before financing, how has this been financed? In LMN's case the net outflow of £26 million in year 3 has been largely financed by borrowings. Given LMN's previous zero level of gearing this may not be a problem. However, the remainder of the outflow has been financed by a decrease in cash. This may cause problems because more cash is usually needed to support increased activity.

However, remember the earlier comment that it is important not to read too much into one year's cash flows because they are so volatile.

- If the net cash flow from operating activities is consistently failing to contribute towards capital expenditure, or if borrowings are steadily increasing (or if cash is steadily decreasing), we would usually expect to see the company reducing its outflow on capital expenditure. With only two years' figures available for LMN, it is not possible to comment on this aspect of their cash management.

7.6 Summary

1. Gearing refers to the proportion of a company's funds that is provided by finance sources on which fixed interest is payable. High gearing can result in wide fluctuations in shareholders' earnings.
2. There are many limitations in the use of ratio analysis. Therefore the analysis should be applied thoughtfully and not mechanically.
3. Cash flows are volatile. Therefore it is important to look at cash-flow trends, and not to read too much into one or two years' cash-flow figures.

Review questions

1. What is financial gearing, and what are the implications of a relatively high gearing ratio? (section 7.2.1)
2. What is the difference between return on shareholders' funds and ROCE? (section 7.3.1)
3. What is meant by 'earnings'? (section 7.3.4)
4. What is the significance of a relatively high PE ratio? (section 7.3.6)
5. State three limitations of ratio analysis based on published financial statements. (section 7.4)
6. State two general guidelines that can be used in performing an outline assessment of a company's published cash-flow statement. (section 7.5)

Self-test questions

1. Refer to question 2 at the end of the previous chapter.

   Required:

   (a) Use the profit and loss accounts and balance sheets to calculate the following for year 7 and year 8 for RC Limited.
      (i) Gearing ratio
      (ii) Interest cover
      (iii) Return on equity
      (iv) Ordinary dividend cover
      (v) Earnings per share

   (b) Comment on the results of your calculations

2. The PE ratios for two companies in the same industry are as follows

	31 March Year 2	31 March Year 3
Company A	9.5	14.6
Company B	10.8	12.9

   What broad conclusions can be drawn from this information?

Answers to self-test questions

1. (a)

		Year 7	Year 8

$$\text{Gearing ratio} = \frac{\text{fixed interest capital}}{\text{total capital employed}} \times 100\% \qquad \frac{25}{106} \times 100\% = 24\% \qquad \frac{40}{135} \times 100\% = 30\%$$

$$\text{Interest cover} = \frac{\text{profit before interest}}{\text{interest payable}} \qquad \frac{36}{4} = 9 \text{ times} \qquad \frac{37}{6} = 6 \text{ times}$$

$$\text{Return on equity} = \frac{\text{net profit after tax}}{\text{ordinary shares} + \text{reserves}} \times 100\% \qquad \frac{24}{81} \times 100\% = 30\% \qquad \frac{24}{95} \times 100\% = 25\%$$

		Year 7	Year 8

$$\text{Ordinary dividend cover} = \frac{\text{net profit after tax}}{\text{ordinary dividend}} \qquad \frac{24}{15} = 1.6 \text{ times} \qquad \frac{24}{10} = 2.4 \text{ times}$$

$$\text{Earnings per share} = \frac{\text{net profit after tax}}{\text{number of ord. shares}} \qquad \frac{24}{50} = 48 \text{ pence} \qquad \frac{24}{50} = 48 \text{ pence}$$

(b) (i) The gearing ratio has increased due to the introduction of more loan capital. This will increase the financial risk associated with the company, and the commitment to pay interest may cause problems if sales continue to fall.

(ii) The interest cover has reduced because the interest cost increased by more than the operating profit.

(iii) The return on equity reduced because the same earnings were achieved but the shareholders' funds increased, due to the retention of year 7 profits.

(iv) The increase in dividend cover is a direct reflection of the reduction in dividend payments for year 8.

(v) There was no change in the earnings per share. The wealth created for each share was the same in both years.

2. The PE ratios for both companies increased in year 3. This indicates a greater confidence generally in the future earning power of companies in this industry. Confidence in the future prospects of company B was higher in year 2, but during year 3 the confidence in company A's prospects grew. By 31 March, year 3 company A's future prospects were viewed more favourably than those of company B.

Part 3

Using financial information to manage a business

Management accounting as an aid to management

8.1 Introduction

In the remainder of this book we will be looking at the financial information which is necessary to help managers to run the business, i.e. we will be discussing the internal management accounts which are not usually made available to the public. In this chapter we will be reviewing the need for management accounting information and discussing the differences between financial accounting and management accounting.

8.2 The need for detailed management accounting information

The financial information that you have learned about so far in this book has been in aggregate form. However, aggregate profit and loss accounts and balance sheets prepared on an historical cost basis do not provide the answers to questions such as the following.

- What did it cost to operate Department A last period?
- What will it cost to operate Department B next period?
- If we decide to close Department C and instead subcontract the work undertaken in that department, what will be the effect on the organisation's total cost?
- Should we accept this order for a batch of product X?
- What price should we charge for a delivery from London to Edinburgh?

The financial accounting information that we have reviewed so far will not help managers to answer these questions. More detailed and forward-looking information is needed and this need is met by an organisation's management accounting system. The management accounting department provides an internal information service to managers to help them to manage.

8.3 The core activities of management accounting

The main activities of the management accounting function could be described as follows:

- **Participation in the planning process at both strategic and operational levels.** In Chapter 11 we will be reviewing the role of financial budgets in the planning process.

- **The initiation of and the provision of guidance for management decisions.** Chapters 9 and 10 will demonstrate how cost information can be analysed to assist managers in their decision-making role.

- **Contributing to the monitoring and control of performance through the provision of reports on organisational (and organisational segment) performance.** Chapter 11 will discuss the use of budgetary control reports to monitor and control the organisation's performance.

8.4 Management accounting compared with financial accounting

Before beginning our discussion of the provision of cost information as a basis for management decisions, it will be useful to review the differences between the financial accounting information that we have covered so far in this book and the management accounting information which we will be considering in the remaining chapters.

The differences between management accounting and financial accounting stem from the different information needs of the people who are using the two types of information.

 If you have forgotten who might be included in the wide range of users of accounts, refer to Chapter 1 of this book to refresh your memory.

The main differences could be summarised as follows:

- **Management accounting reports are for internal use only.** Financial accounts are prepared to satisfy the information needs of a variety of users both internal and external to the business.

- **Management accounting reports are usually very detailed.** If they are to be effective in supporting managers in the decision-making process, many management accounting reports need to be provided in considerable detail. Financial accounting statements provide an aggregated overview of an organisation's performance.

- ***Management accounting reports often provide forecast information as well as historical information.*** Management accounting tends to be more forward-looking whereas financial accounting statements are largely historical, providing information about past performance. However, certain types of financial accounting reports may contain projected information. For example, a company might issue forecasts to external users when it is attempting to raise more capital.

- ***Management accounting reports are not regulated by external bodies.*** Because they are prepared for internal use only, management accounting reports may contain any information which is useful for the managers who are to use it. This information may be presented in any way that suits the needs of the organisation, and there are no external regulations to restrict this freedom. In contrast, financial accounting statements must conform with the accounting requirements of the Companies' Acts, as well as with the recommendations contained in Financial Reporting Standards and Statements of Standard Accounting Practice. These regulations are designed to protect the external users of financial accounts, so that they can be sure that all organisations' accounts are prepared on a standardised basis.

 In most companies the production of management accounts (and many other aspects of the business) is regulated by internal audit departments – which can be more rigorous in their investigations than many external bodies!

- ***Many management accounting reports are prepared for a specific, one-off purpose.*** For example, a management accounting report may be prepared to help with a particular decision, or a report might be addressed to and designed for a particular manager within the organisation. Financial accounting reports tend to be more general-purpose. Most are prepared on a regular, routine basis and they are designed to be useful to a wide range of potential users.

- ***Management accounting reports tend to be produced more frequently than financial accounting reports.*** Most organisations publish their financial accounts once a year in their annual report. Many also publish abbreviated interim reports on a half-yearly or quarterly basis. In contrast, management accounting reports can be prepared monthly, weekly, or even daily to allow managers to monitor current results on a regular basis.

8.5 Summary

1. Management accounting provides the detailed, forward-looking information that managers need to help them to manage the business.

2. Management accounting contains three core activities: participation in the planning process, the initiation of and the provision of guidance for management decisions, and contributing to the monitoring and control of performance.

3. A number of differences can be identified between management accounting and financial accounting. These differences stem from the different information needs of the people who are using the two types of information.

The analysis of cost

9.1 Introduction

This chapter will explore a fundamental issue in management accounting: what is meant by cost? We will be looking at the different measures of cost and at what makes up the total cost of a product or service. You will also be learning about overhead absorption, which is the process of determining the overhead cost of a product or service.

9.2 The elements of cost

9.2.1 What makes up total cost?

Imagine that you work as a salesperson for a company that manufactures and sells wall-mounted hairdryers: the type that are fixed to the wall for customers' use in hotel bedrooms. You have been negotiating with the procurement manager of a chain of hotels in an attempt to secure a contract to supply a batch of hairdryers. It is very important that you should win this contract because it is likely that, once this first order has been fulfiled successfully, the hotel chain will place future orders for hairdryers and for your company's other products, when refurbishing its other hotels. Furthermore, other hotel chains may become interested in your company's products once they discover that this major chain is one of your customers.

Unfortunately the hotel's procurement manager is working within the constraints of a very strict budget and has made it clear that the highest price that the hotel is prepared to pay is £10 per hairdryer. Your company's normal selling price is considerably higher than this.

Undaunted, you go to see your company's management accountant who informs you that this is not an attractive proposition because the company's cost per hairdryer is £12. This seems to be the end of the matter. The company cannot afford to sell its hairdryers for £10 each if they cost £12 to produce. Or can it? If we can find out what makes up this cost of £12 per hairdryer we will be in a better position to make a management decision about this potential order.

The elements of cost are as follows.

	Direct material	
+	Direct labour	
+	Direct expense	
=	Total direct cost or prime cost	
+	Production overhead (share of)	• indirect production materials
		• indirect production labour
		• indirect production expense
=	Total production cost	
+	Other overhead (share of)	• selling and distribution overhead
		• administration overhead
=	Total cost	

Now let us look at the sort of costs that might be incurred in manufacturing and selling a hairdryer, and how each cost would be classified in terms of the above analysis of the elements of cost.

- **Direct materials**. This is the material that actually becomes part of the finished hairdryer. It would include the plastic for the case and the packaging materials. If we make another batch of hairdryers then we will need to purchase another batch of these and other direct materials.
- **Direct labour**. This is the labour cost incurred directly as a result of making one hairdryer. Direct labour cost is not so common nowadays because many employees are paid a guaranteed wage regardless of their level of output. This guaranteed wage would not be classified as a direct labour cost in this case because it is not directly caused by the manufacture of any individual hairdryer. However, our manufacturing staff may be paid a bonus of, say, £1 per hairdryer produced, in addition to their guaranteed wage. This bonus would be a direct labour cost because one more batch of hairdryers would lead to the payment of more £1 bonuses.
- **Direct expenses**. These are expenses caused directly as a result of making one more batch of hairdryers. For example, it might include the cost of the power to run the machinery to produce the batch for the hotel chain.

The three direct costs are totalled to derive the prime cost or total direct cost of a hairdryer. This is one measure of cost but there are still other costs to be added: production overheads and other overheads.

Production overheads are basically the same three costs as for direct cost, but they are identified as *indirect* costs because they cannot be specifically identified with any particular hairdryer or batch of hairdryers. Indirect costs must be shared out over all the production using a fair and equitable basis.

Later in this chapter you will see how indirect costs can be shared over all the production for the period.

Indirect materials are those production materials that do not actually become part of the finished product. This might include the cleaning materials and lubricating oils for the machinery. The machines must be clean and lubricated in order to carry out production, but it will probably not be necessary to spend more on these materials in order to manufacture a further batch. This cost is therefore only indirectly related to the production of this batch.

Indirect labour is the production labour cost which cannot be directly associated with the production of any particular batch. It would include the guaranteed wage that was mentioned earlier, and the salaries of supervisors who are overseeing the production of hairdryers as well as all the other products manufactured in the factory.

Indirect expenses are all the other production overheads associated with running the factory, including factory rent and rates, heating and lighting, etc. These indirect costs must be shared out over all of the output in a period. The share of indirect production costs is added to the prime cost to derive the total production cost of a hairdryer. This is another measure of cost but there are still more costs to be added: a share of the other overheads.

Selling and distribution overhead includes the sales force salaries and commission, the cost of operating delivery vehicles and renting a storage warehouse, etc. Most of this cost must be shared over all of the products sold in a period.

Administration overhead includes the rent on the administrative office building, the depreciation of office equipment, postage and stationery costs, etc. This cost must again be shared over all the products produced.

Now that you understand the nature of each of the cost elements which make up total cost we can return to our management accountant and ask for a detailed breakdown of the total cost of £12.

Total cost of a hairdryer

		£
	Direct material	4
+	Direct labour	2
+	Direct expense	1
=	Total direct cost or prime cost	7
+	Production overhead (share of)	2
=	Total production cost	9
+	Other overhead (share of)	3
=	Total cost	12

Now we are in a better position to judge the potential effect of accepting an order at a selling price of £10 per hairdryer.

Exercise
Which of the above costs would be incurred as a result of making a further batch of hairdryers?

Solution
The direct cost of £7 would definitely be incurred if another batch was produced. This is the extra material that would have to be bought, the extra labour bonuses that would have to be paid and the extra expenses for power, etc. that would be incurred.

The £2 production overhead cost would not be incurred if another batch was produced. This is the share of costs that would be incurred anyway, such as the cleaning materials, the factory rent and the supervisors' salaries.

The £3 share of 'other' overhead would probably not be incurred if another batch was produced. This includes the office costs, the depreciation on the delivery vehicles and the rent of warehousing facilities. This sort of cost would not increase as a result of producing another batch. However, there may be some incremental or extra selling and distribution costs, for example we would probably be entitled to a sales commission for all our hard work in winning the sale, and there would be some costs involved in delivering the batch to the hotel chain. For the sake of our analysis let us suppose that this incremental cost amounts to £1 per hairdryer, rather than the full amount of £3 shown in the cost breakdown.

You can see from the discussion in this exercise that in fact the only extra cost to be incurred in producing a further batch of hairdryers is £8 per hairdryer (£7 direct cost + assumed £1 extra selling and distribution costs). Therefore it may be possible to sell to the hotel chain for £10 per hairdryer, and still be better off than if the sale was not made at all! At least the extra £2 per hairdryer (£10 – £8 extra cost) would contribute towards the costs which are being incurred anyway – the production overheads, administration overheads, etc.

In the next chapter you will see that the costs which would be incurred anyway and which would not be affected by the manufacture of a further batch are called the fixed costs. The costs which would increase in line with the number of batches produced are called the variable costs.

9.2.2 The need for subjective judgement

This exercise has demonstrated how more detailed cost information can help managers to make better-informed decisions. You should also appreciate that, although more information improves the ability to make the decision, it still cannot replace the need for management to exercise judgement.

Exercise

It seems that for commercial reasons it may be worth while selling a batch of hairdryers to the hotel chain for less than the normal selling price. But what other factors do you think managers should consider before agreeing to the sale?

Solution

You may have thought of the following factors, as well as others which would be equally worth consideration:

- Can the batch be produced without affecting the remainder of our production, i.e. can it be fitted onto our existing facilities? If full-price business had to be displaced, or if overtime payments were incurred, this would increase the incremental cost of producing the batch.
- Will we be committing ourselves to charging this price on all business with the hotel, or is it a 'low introductory price'? Otherwise we could find that, as our level of business with the hotel grows, more and more of our sales are being priced at this low level and we will not be earning enough contribution toward the indirect, shared costs.
- Will our existing 'full-price' customers find out that we are selling to the hotel at a lower price, and begin to demand a discount as well?

9.2.3 A second example

Before we leave the subject of direct versus indirect cost, it will be worth while working through another exercise. This will ensure that you are completely clear about what constitutes a direct cost and what is an indirect cost. This time we will look at a service organisation.

Exercise

Spotless Limited is an office cleaning business which employs a team of part-time cleaners who are paid an hourly wage. The business provides cleaning services for a number of clients, from small offices attached to high street shops to large open-plan offices in high-rise buildings.

In determining the cost of providing a cleaning service to a particular client, which of the following costs would be a direct cost of cleaning that client's office and which would be an indirect cost?

(a) The wages paid to the cleaner who is sent to the client's premises

(b) The cost of carpet shampoo used by the cleaner

(c) The salaries of Spotless Limited's accounts clerks

(d) Rent of the premises where Spotless Limited stores its cleaning materials and equipment

(e) Travelling expenses paid to the cleaner to reach the client's premises

(f) Advertising expenses incurred in attracting more clients to Spotless Limited's business

Solution

The direct costs are (a), (b) and (e) because they can be directly identified with this particular client. The other costs are indirect because they would have to be shared among all of the clients serviced by Spotless Limited.

9.3 Overhead absorption

The process of sharing out the indirect costs over a number of products or services is called overhead absorption or overhead recovery. You will appreciate that this can be a very arbitrary task. For example, in the previous exercise, who can say how much of the accounts clerks' salaries should be allocated to each client?

It may be easiest to simply divide the total salary cost by the number of clients to derive a cost per client. However, this may not reflect the true cost of servicing each client, and later in this chapter we will see how the absorption of overheads can be more sophisticated than this simple division.

9.3.1 Why do we absorb overheads?

We have seen that the absorption or sharing out of overheads can at times be rather arbitrary. We have also seen that in certain management decisions these absorbed costs are not relevant, and that management will often focus on the direct costs and not place so much importance on the indirect costs.

So why do we bother to undertake the task of absorption at all? Why not simply concentrate on the direct costs which can be allocated to products and services reasonably accurately?

There are two main reasons why we might need to calculate the fully absorbed cost of a product or service:

- *To have an understanding of the long-run average cost of our products and services.* This can be useful in many decisions, including pricing. Some organisations will take the total cost and add a percentage to this to determine their selling price. This is known as 'cost-plus' pricing but it can be a difficult practice to follow in a competitive market. In this type of market a supplier may have to set prices according to what customers are prepared to pay, rather than according to what the supplier would like to charge!

In our example of the hairdryer manufacturer in this chapter, a cost-plus price would have been determined by adding a percentage profit mark-up to the total cost of £12. However, this was not possible in the case of the potential order from the hotel chain – the market was attempting to dictate the price here.

- **To match cost against revenue when calculating profit.** In your studies of financial accounting in the earlier chapters of this book you saw how the correct costs should be matched against each item of revenue to determine the profit for the period. Therefore if any stock is carried forward at the end of a period the full cost of this stock must be determined, including a fair share of overhead, so that the correct total cost can be matched against the sales revenue when the stock items are sold in a later period.

This matching of costs also occurs in service industries. For example, a systems analyst may be designing a computer system for an organisation, and the system might not be completed at the end of the period, therefore no revenue will yet have been earned. It would not be fair to charge the development and overhead costs incurred to date in this year's profit and loss account. Instead the full cost of the work done to date may be carried over and charged against the revenue which is earned in a later period when the system is completed. It is the management accountant's task to determine this full cost so that profit measurement is not distorted.

This is an example of work in progress – you learned about it in Chapter 3. The value of the work in progress would be shown as a current asset in the balance sheet at the end of the period.

9.3.2 Absorbing overheads: traditional basis

We will now move on to look at how production overheads might be absorbed, i.e. shared out between products and services, in practice. We will begin by looking at the more traditional methods which are used to absorb overheads. Then we will go on to consider the criticisms of these methods in the modern operating environment, before reviewing more modern approaches to absorption costing.

Thinking back to our example of the hairdryer manufacturer, the types of indirect production cost that we described there were as follows:

- *Indirect materials*: cleaning materials and lubricating oils
- *Indirect labour*: basic wage of production employees, supervisors' salaries
- *Indirect expenses*: factory rent and rates, factory heating and lighting.

A simple way of sharing out these overheads would be as follows:

$$\text{Overhead charge per hairdryer} = \frac{\text{Total production overheads in period}}{\text{Number of hairdryers produced in period}}$$

This method would work perfectly well if the company simply produced identical hairdryers all the time, and nothing else. However, this is not the case in this example and rarely is it the case in practice. It is unusual to find an organisation that produces homogeneous products that are similar in size and complexity. It is more likely that a range of products is produced, each of which places a different burden on the production facilities and which should each therefore carry a different amount of production overhead.

Looking at all the indirect costs described it could be argued that each of them tends to increase with time. The longer a machine is operated, the more lubricating oils and cleaning materials will be consumed. The longer a factory operates, the higher will be the salary and heating costs, etc.

The traditional methods of overhead absorption are based on the assumption that most overheads accrue with the passage of time. Therefore it makes sense that the longer an item takes to produce, the more overheads it should be charged, because it will have placed a greater burden on the factory facilities.

One measure of time taken is direct labour hours. Using this basis an overhead absorption rate can be calculated as follows:

$$\text{Overhead absorption rate per direct labour hour} = \frac{\text{Total production overheads in period}}{\text{Total direct labour hours in period}}$$

9.3.3 Using a direct labour hour rate to absorb overheads: example

The best way to see how to apply this absorption method is to work through an example.

Tronics Limited repairs and services specialist sports cars. Overheads incurred are £27,000 per period. Tronics absorbs overheads using a direct labour hour rate. During each period the total number of direct labour hours worked on servicing and repairs is 6,000. The following data relates to the repair job number 376.

Parts and spares used	£287
Direct labour charged to job (5 hours)	£ 40

Use this data to calculate the total cost of job number 376.

The first thing we will need to do is to calculate the overhead absorption rate:

$$\text{Overhead absorption rate per direct labour hour} = \frac{\text{£27,000}}{6,000} = \text{£4.50 per labour hour}$$

This means that every time a labour hour is worked on a job, £4.50 will be charged to the job as its share of the overheads for the period. Over the whole period, 6000 hours will be charged to jobs at an overhead rate of £4.50 per hour, so the total charges made for overhead will amount to 6,000 ∞ £4.50 = £27,000. The overhead will have been charged to the jobs as fairly as possible, using a time-based method. Jobs that have a lot of labour hours charged to them will be charged a higher share of the overhead than jobs which incur fewer labour hours.

We can now determine the total cost of repair job number 376:

	£
Parts and spares used	287.00
Direct labour charged to job (5 hours)	40.00
Prime cost	327.00
Overhead (5 labour hours x £4.50 per hour)	22.50
Total cost	349.50

Note that the prime cost for the job would remain unaltered whichever method was chosen to absorb overheads.

Exercise

Fine Furniture Limited manufactures pine bedroom furniture. The expected costs to be incurred on all orders next period are as follows:

	£
Direct materials – wood	3,800
– screws, glue, etc.	250
Indirect materials	300
Direct labour	5,600
Supervisor's salary	2,300
Depreciation of machinery	200
Rent and rates	1,200
Electricity and gas	400
Telephone	150
Other overheads	250

Overheads are to be absorbed using a direct labour hour rate. A total of 800 labour hours will be worked during the next period.

A customer has requested a quotation for a king-size pine bed. The wood for the bed will cost £180 and other direct material cost will be £10. Direct labour hours will amount to 12 hours at a labour cost of £84. What will be the total cost of this order?

Solution

Total overhead = indirect materials £300 + supervisor's salary £2300 + depreciation £200 + rent and rates £1200 + electricity and gas £400 + telephone £150 + other £250 = £4,800

$$\text{Direct labour hour rate for overhead absorption} = \frac{£4,800}{800 \text{ hours}} = £6 \text{ per labour hour}$$

Cost of king size bed:	£
Direct materials	190
Direct labour	84
Prime cost	274
Overheads 12 hours x £6	72
Total cost	346

9.3.4 Absorbing overheads based on machine hours

Another time-based absorption rate that is widely used is a machine hour rate. This works in exactly the same way as a direct labour hour rate, except that the absorption is based on the number of machine hours taken to produce each item. The machine hour rate would be calculated as follows:

$$\text{Overhead absorption rate per machine hour} = \frac{\text{Total production overheads in period}}{\text{Total machine hours in period}}$$

The machine time would be recorded for each item produced. The number of machine hours would be multiplied by the machine hour rate of overhead absorption, as calculated using the above formula, to derive the overhead cost for the item.

This method is obviously most suitable when production is more mechanised. In a mechanised environment many overheads will be related to the number of machine hours used.

Exercise

Can you think of types of overhead cost that would tend to be higher when production is highly mechanised?

Solution

You may have thought of the following costs.

- Depreciation of machinery
- Power costs
- Indirect materials: lubricating oils, etc.
- Insurance of machinery
- Machinery maintenance costs

143

9.3.5 Departmental overhead absorption rates

The examples we have seen so far calculated a single rate of overhead absorption to be applied to all production. However, in practice an organisation might be divided into many different departments which undertake various activities to produce the final output. For example, for Fine Furniture Limited a king-size bed might pass through the following departments during the production process:

Cutting department   – the wood is cut to size
↓
Joining department   – the wood is joined by skilled carpenters
↓
Finishing department   – the bed is finished, the edges are smoothed, etc.
↓
Packing department   – the bed is packed in cardboard ready for
                    despatch to the customer

The rate of incidence of overhead in each department is likely to be different. Some departments would incur a higher level of overhead and others would have a low level. Furthermore, it is possible that, over the range of products manufactured by Fine Furniture Limited, certain products would spend longer in some departments than in others. Therefore the overhead charge would represent a more accurate reflection of the burden placed on the facilities if a separate charge was made for each department.

To further complicate matters, perhaps the cutting department is machine intensive whereas the other three departments might be more labour intensive. Therefore a machine hour rate would be most appropriate in the cutting department, with a labour hour rate being used in the other three departments.

In a system which uses departmental absorption rates the overhead would be recorded separately for each department, as would the hours worked on production, i.e. machine hours in the cutting department and labour hours in the other three departments. A separate hourly rate would be calculated for each department with the result that a product which passes through all four departments would be charged with four separate amounts of overhead, i.e. one for each department, based on the time taken in each department.

Exercise

Separate departmental hourly rates of overhead absorption have now been determined for the forthcoming period for Fine Furniture Limited:

Cutting department	£7 per machine hour
Joining department	£5 per direct labour hour
Finishing department	£6 per direct labour hour
Packing department	£4 per direct labour hour

The proposed order for the king-size pine bed will require the following hours in each department:

Cutting department	3 machine hours
Joining department	6 direct labour hours
Finishing department	2 direct labour hours
Packing department	1 direct labour hour

The estimated prime cost for the order will remain as before, i.e. £274. What is the revised total cost of the king-size bed?

Solution

Cost of king-size bed	£	£
Direct materials		190
Direct labour		84
Prime cost		274
Overhead cost		
cutting dept (3 hours x £7)	21	
joining dept (6 hours x £5)	30	
finishing dept (2 hours x £6)	12	
packing dept (1 hour x £4)	4	
		67
Total cost		341

The use of separate departmental overhead absorption rates has led to a lower overhead charge for this particular order. However, it is important to realise that the same total overhead for Fine Furniture Limited is to be shared over all the products manufactured in the period. Therefore if this particular bed is to absorb a smaller amount of overhead, other products manufactured in the period will absorb a higher amount of overhead than they would have done using the single absorption rate. The overall result will be the same. The total overhead for the period will be absorbed by all the output or production.

9.3.6 Using predetermined overhead absorption rates

You may have noticed that in all the exercises and examples we have been calculating the overhead absorption rates for the forthcoming period, i.e. we have been using predetermined absorption rates. Predetermined rates are used for the following reasons:

- Managers need to have an overhead rate readily available throughout the period for quotations, cost estimates, etc. It would be very time consuming to have to calculate a new rate several times during the period and managers would not be able to wait until the end of the period to see what the overhead rate should be. Therefore the rate is estimated in advance for the forthcoming period.
- Overhead costs tend to be incurred at uneven time intervals. For example, gas and telephone bills are paid quarterly whereas rent and salary bills may be paid monthly. The result would be very high overhead rates in some weeks and very low overhead rates in others. Calculating an overall rate for a longer period smooths out these fluctuations in timing.

Clearly, the actual overhead rate will often turn out to be different from the predetermined rate that has been applied throughout the period. Therefore the overheads that have been absorbed into production will be higher or lower than the actual overheads incurred. The difference between the two amounts is called the over- or under-absorbed overhead.

 This might happen if the actual overhead expenditure is different from forecast, and/or if the actual hours are different from forecast. If more overhead is absorbed than was incurred, this is called an over-absorption. The opposite situation is called an under-absorption.

An adjustment for this under- or over-absorption can be made in the accounts at the end of the period. However, it is obviously undesirable for the over- or under-absorption to be very high, otherwise managers have been using very inaccurate cost rates as a basis for pricing and other decisions during the period. This situation can be avoided by regular reviews of the absorption rates throughout the period, to check that they are as accurate as possible at all times.

9.4 Recent developments in absorption costing methods

9.4.1 The criticisms of the traditional approach

Historically, the most common methods of absorbing production overhead have been based on an hourly rate, either labour hours or machine hours, for reasons discussed earlier in this chapter. However, the nature of the competitive environment is changing for many companies. The result is that customer needs are changing more rapidly and their requirements are becoming more complex.

For example, Fine Furniture Limited may previously have found that, apart from small changes required in the size of their pine beds, their output was fairly standard and that operations were reasonably standardised. However, more recently they may have been receiving requests for different-shaped headboards on the beds, perhaps with personalised carvings. Responding to these more complex and individual requirements results in a much more complex operation. Not only is it more difficult to produce the bed, but the liaison with the customer becomes more involved and the quality control activity needs to be redesigned.

The end result is that overheads are not necessarily incurred in relation to the actual time taken to produce the bed. Instead overheads are incurred in relation to the relative complexity of the activities that have to be undertaken during all the dealings with the customer, right from the first receipt of the request for a quotation to the receipt of payment from the customer.

Exercise

Can you think of, say, three additional activities that would have to be undertaken within Fine Furniture Limited as the result of a customer's order for a bed with a personalised carved headboard?

Solution

You may have thought of activities such as the following:

- Initial liaison with the customer to ascertain the exact design required.
- Consultation with a specialist carver to determine the cost of personalisation.
- Quality control checking to ensure that the product meets the specific customer requirements.
- Separate stock control procedures for non-standard items.
- Invoice checking to ensure that the customer is charged for the specialist services received.

The traditional overhead absorption methods based on time taken are not sufficiently flexible to deal with such complexity in the modern operating environment. One method that has been developed to attempt to cope with this complexity is activity-based costing.

9.4.2 Activity-based costing

Activity-based costing (ABC) analyses all the activities undertaken by an organisation to identify what drives the costs incurred, i.e. what causes the costs to increase. These cost drivers may be labour hours or machine hours but they could also be a variety of other factors.

For example, an analysis of quality control activity might identify that quality control costs are driven by the number of special customer requests, i.e. the higher the number of special requests, the higher are the quality control costs. Therefore a relatively standard product would not be associated with a high incidence of the cost driver 'specific requests' and so would receive a relatively low charge for quality control overhead. A product which involved a high number of 'specific requests' would be charged a relatively high amount of the quality control cost.

The strength of an activity-based costing system is that it can be applied to all overhead costs incurred, and not just to the production overheads which are traditionally absorbed using a time-based method. Look back to the question that was posed at the beginning of section 9.3. 'Who can say how much of the accounts clerks' salaries should be allocated to each client?'

Using an activity-based analysis, it might be possible to identify what *drives* the cost of employing accounts clerks in an office cleaning business. For example, we might ask the simple question 'what causes an accounts clerk to become more busy and in what circumstances would it be necessary to employ more accounts clerks?' By asking these questions we are attempting to determine the *cost drivers* for the activities undertaken by the accounts clerks.

We might be surprised to learn that perhaps it is not the number of clients which drives costs, but some other factor. For example, our accounts clerks might tell us that they are made more busy when the company takes on larger clients. Larger clients might mean that they need to process and account for more requisitions for materials, they have to account for the hiring of more heavy-duty cleaning equipment, and perhaps larger clients require more attention in terms of credit control!

An easily measured cost driver for the accounts clerks' salaries might therefore be 'square metres of floor space to be cleaned' rather than 'number of clients'. Larger clients would then be charged with more of the accounts clerks' salaries and smaller clients would be charged less. This would lead to a better analysis of cost and therefore better information for managers to use in their day-to-day control of the business.

9.4.3 The development of activity-based analysis

In the early days of ABC it was most widely adopted in manufacturing organisations. However, it also has general applicability and is being used in the service sector. Surveys have shown that ABC is being adopted, or at least experimented with, in various types of service organisation ranging from hospitals to financial service organisations.

The following extract is taken from Cornhill Insurance plc's annual report for 1996:

'A system of activity-based product costing has been developed to refine our allocation of expenses by product. The concept was found to be beneficial in UK Branch division and is now being introduced into other trading areas.'

On the other hand, ABC should not be viewed as a panacea for all product costing problems. Many critics of ABC argue that the determination of cost drivers is too complicated and time consuming and the cost involved outweighs any benefits that might be derived from the improved cost allocation.

9.5 Summary

1. The total cost of a product or service is made up of its direct cost plus a share of indirect costs or overheads.
2. The process of assigning overheads to products or services is known as overhead absorption.
3. Overhead absorption has traditionally used direct labour hours or machine hours as an absorption basis.
4. Recent developments in overhead absorption techniques attempt to identify what drives overhead costs in order to determine more appropriate bases for overhead allocation.

Review questions
1. What are the elements of cost? (section 9.2.1)
2. Why is overhead absorption necessary? (section 9.3.1)
3. Why has overhead absorption traditionally been based on time? (section 9.3.2)
4. Explain how a direct labour hour rate is used to absorb overheads. (section 9.3.3)
5. Why are overhead absorption rates determined in advance of each period? (section 9.3.6)
6. What is a cost driver? (section 9.4.2)

Self-test question

S Limited manufactures self-assembly garden sheds and log cabins to cus-tomers' individual requirements. Forecast production overhead costs for the forthcoming period are:

	£
Indirect labour	20,000
Rent and rates	12,000
Electricity and gas	4,500
Indirect material	2,200
Machine running costs (7,000 hours)	8,800
Other indirect production costs	1,500

S Ltd adds ten per cent to the total production of each job, in order to absorb non-production overheads.

A customer has ordered a log cabin, job number 771, which will incur the following costs.

Direct material	£400
Direct labour	£180
Machine running time	8 hours

What is the total cost of job number 771?

Answer to self-test question

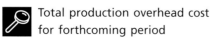

Total production overhead cost
for forthcoming period   = £49,000

Production overhead cost per
machine running hour   = £49,000 / 7,000
                             = £7 per machine hour

Total cost of job 771	£
Direct material	400.00
Direct labour	180.00
Total direct cost	580.00
Production overheads (8 hour x £7)	56.00
Total production cost	636.00
Non-production overheads 10%	63.60
Total cost	699.60

0 Using costs for decision-making

10.1 Introduction

In this chapter you will find out more about how costs can be used to assist managers in their decision-making activities. You will learn about cost behaviour patterns and about different classifications of cost for decision-making, including relevant costs and opportunity costs.

10.2 Cost behaviour patterns

The term 'cost behaviour patterns' is used to describe the way in which costs behave in relation to the level of activity. For example the question 'does this cost increase in line with activity or does it remain constant?' is the same as asking 'what is the cost behaviour pattern for this cost?'

A variety of different factors can cause costs to increase or change, for example inflation or a scarcity in supply. However, in management accounting, when we talk about cost behaviour patterns we mean the way that they behave in relation to the level of activity. Activity can be measured in a variety of ways depending on the organisation, the type of cost being analysed and the reason for analysing the cost. Common measures of activity include the level of sales, the level of production, number of customers, number of employees, etc.

10.2.1 Fixed costs

A fixed cost is one which tends to be unaffected by fluctuations in the level of activity. Figure 10.1 shows a fixed cost of £10,000.

Figure 10.1: Fixed cost

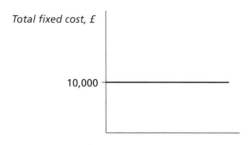

Notice that the total cost incurred in the period is £10,000 for all activity levels, even at zero activity. Therefore in the short term, an organisation will have to pay all its fixed bills, even if activity drops to zero.

Another term which is sometimes used to describe a fixed cost is a period cost. This highlights the fact that a fixed cost is incurred according to the time elapsed, rather than according to the level of activity.

Exercise

Can you name two costs that are likely to be fixed costs for a small restaurant business?

Solution

You may have thought of costs such as the following:

- Rent and rates
- Salaries of kitchen staff
- Insurance
- Depreciation of equipment

Looking at the costs listed in this solution, they will all tend to be unaffected by the number of customers served in a period. However, you have probably realised that there may come a point when the business has expanded so much that more kitchen staff are needed to cope with the demand, or perhaps bigger premises will be necessary. There will then be corresponding increases in the costs of salaries, rent and rates, etc. So how can we describe these as fixed costs?

A fixed cost will be unaffected by activity changes *within a relevant range of activity*. If activity extends beyond this range then the identified fixed cost behaviour pattern may not be applicable. Figure 10.2 demonstrates this.

Figure 10.2: Stepped fixed cost

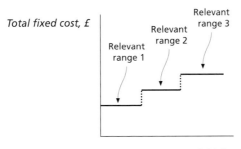

Activity level

This could be depicting the cost of kitchen staff's salaries. The cost remains fixed for a certain range of activity. Within this range it is possible to serve more customers without needing extra kitchen staff and therefore the salary cost remains constant. However, if activity is expanded to the critical point where another staff member is needed then the salary cost increases to a new, higher level. The cost then remains constant for a further range of increases in activity until another staff member is needed and another step occurs, and so on.

The possibility of changes occurring in cost behaviour patterns means that it is unreliable to attempt to predict costs for activity levels which are outside the relevant range. For example, our records might show the staff levels needed at various activity levels between, say, 150 and 250 customers. We should therefore try to avoid using this information as the basis for forecasting the level of cost which would be incurred at an activity of, say, 350 customers, which is outside the relevant range.

 This warning does not apply only to fixed costs. It is never wise to attempt to predict costs for activity levels outside the range for which cost behaviour patterns have been established.

10.2.2 Variable costs

A variable cost is one which varies in line with the level of activity. The higher the level of activity, the higher will be the cost incurred. Figure 10.3 depicts a linear variable cost.

Figure 10.3: Linear variable cost

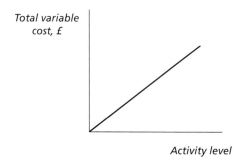

Total variable cost, £

Activity level

The graph is a straight line through the origin which means that the cost is nil at zero activity level. When activity increases the total variable cost increases in direct proportion, i.e. if activity goes up by 10 per cent, then the total variable cost also increases by 10 per cent, as long as the activity level is still within the relevant range.

Exercise

Can you name two costs that are likely to be variable costs for the restaurant business?

Solution

You may have thought of costs such as the following:

• Food
• Laundry costs for napkins and tablecloths

These costs will both tend to increase as the level of activity increases.

In many planning and decision-making situations, variable costs are assumed to be linear. Although many variable costs do approximate to a linear pattern this assumption may not always be realistic.

The important point is that managers should be aware of any assumptions that have been made in estimating cost behaviour patterns. They can then use the information which is based on these assumptions with a full awareness of its possible limitations.

A variable cost may be non-linear as depicted in either of the diagrams in Figure 10.4.

Figure 10.4: Non-linear variable cost

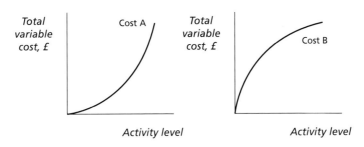

 These costs are sometimes called curvilinear variable costs.

The graph of cost A becomes steeper as the activity level rises. This indicates that each successive unit of activity is adding more to the total variable cost than the previous unit. An example of a variable cost which follows this pattern could be where specialist food ingredients are in short supply and it is necessary to pay higher prices to acquire the larger quantities needed when more customers are served.

The graph of cost B becomes less steep as the activity level increases. Each successive unit of activity adds less to total variable cost than the previous unit. An example of a variable cost which follows this pattern could be the cost of readily obtained food ingredients where quantity discounts are available.

 Exercise

The costs depicted in the figures so far in this chapter have all been total costs over a range of activity. Can you sketch graphs for the following costs over a range of activity?

- Fixed cost per unit
- Variable cost per unit

Solution

Fixed cost per unit:

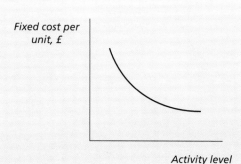

Fixed cost per
unit, £

Activity level

Variable cost per unit:

Variable cost
per unit, £

Activity level

The fixed cost per unit reduces as the activity level is increased. This is because the same amount of fixed cost is being spread over an increasing number of units. For the variable cost per unit, the straight line parallel to the horizontal axis depicts a constant variable cost per unit, within the relevant range.

The similarity between these graphs and those depicted earlier in the chapter should demonstrate to you the importance of reading the labels on the axes before attempting to interpret a graph of a cost behaviour pattern.

10.2.3 Semi-variable costs

A semi-variable cost is also referred to as a semi-fixed or mixed cost. It is a cost which contains both fixed and variable components and which is therefore partly affected by fluctuations in the level of activity. A graph of a semi-variable cost might appear as shown in Figure 10.5.

Figure 10.5: Semi-variable cost

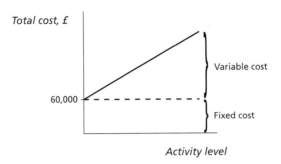

This particular semi-variable cost has a basic fixed component of £60,000 which is incurred even at zero activity. As activity levels increase, a variable component is incurred in addition to the basic fixed cost.

Exercise

Can you name two costs that are likely to be semi-variable costs for the restaurant business?

Solution

You may have thought of costs such as the following.

- Telephone
- Gas
- Electricity

All these costs have a basic fixed component which must be paid irrespective of usage. As activity increases, so does the total cost incurred but the basic fixed element remains the same.

Now that you have learned about the main cost behaviour patterns that are found in business we can look at cost-volume-profit analysis which depends on an understanding of cost behaviour.

10.3 Cost-volume-profit analysis

Cost-volume-profit (CVP) analysis is:

'the study of the effects on future profit of changes in fixed cost, variable cost, sales price, quantity and mix.' CIMA *Official Terminology*

Suppose that you are considering opening your own small restaurant. Before commencing on your new venture you will need to consider many

factors, both financial and non-financial. One key decision factor will probably be: 'How many customers do I need to attract in order to break even
each month?'

With a basic understanding of your likely prices, as well as your costs and
their behaviour patterns, you should be able to estimate your breakeven
point.

10.3.1 Calculating the breakeven point: example

Suppose that you have produced the following estimates of your monthly
costs.

Fixed costs	£ per month
Rent and rates	800
Salaries	4,000
Insurance	115
Other	100
	5,015

Variable costs	£ per customer (average)
Food and beverages	5
Laundry	2
Other	1
	8

 *Notice that the fixed costs are expressed in terms of the amount for a time period,
whereas variable costs are expressed in relation to a unit of activity, i.e. a customer.*

You have also estimated that the average income from each customer will
be £25.

We can now calculate the breakeven point. The first step is to calculate
the contribution from each customer.

Every time we serve a customer we receive £25 and we have to pay out
£8 for food, etc. The management accounting term for this difference of £17
is the 'contribution'. Therefore we earn a contribution of £17 per customer:

Sales income less variable costs = contribution

£25 – £8 = £17

This amount is called the contribution because it literally does contribute
towards the fixed costs which we incur no matter how many customers we
serve. Therefore if we have one customer we have £17 contribution towards
the fixed costs of £5,015. If we have two customers we have £34 contribution
towards the fixed costs, and so on.

To break even we need just sufficient contribution to pay all the fixed costs. Then we will have nothing left: no profit and no loss, i.e. we will have reached the breakeven point:

$$\text{Breakeven point} = \frac{\text{Fixed costs}}{\text{Contribution per customer}} = \frac{£5,015}{£17}$$

$$= 295 \text{ customers per month}$$

10.3.2 Margin of safety

Now that we have an estimate of the breakeven point for our proposed business we can start to think about whether it seems to be a sound proposition. Based on our knowledge of the potential customer demand for our restaurant, we can calculate the margin of safety.

The margin of safety is the difference between what we need to achieve to break even and what we believe we can achieve. The larger the margin of safety, the more likely we are to be able to earn some sort of profit. Suppose that we predict that we will be able to attract, on average, 400 customers each month.

Forecast level of demand less breakeven level of demand = margin of safety

400 – 295 = 105 customers

This means that we can afford to attract 105 fewer customers than we are estimating, before we begin to make losses in any one month, i.e. our margin of safety is approximately 26 per cent of our forecast demand.

Percentage margin of safety =

$^{105}/_{400}$ x 100% = 26%

Exercise
What factors do you think would affect your assessment of whether this was an adequate safety margin for your forecast demand?

Solution
• What is your attitude to risk?
• How accurate is the demand forecast likely to be, i.e. is your knowledge of the market so poor that you could well have overestimated demand by 26 per cent?
• How accurate are your estimates of cost and revenue?

The margin of safety also helps us to calculate the likely monthly profit for our restaurant business. Once the breakeven point has been reached, each customer's contribution will go towards profit, because there are no more fixed bills to pay.

Therefore the monthly profit from 400 customers per month can be forecast as follows:

105 customers above breakeven x £17 contribution per customer = £1,785

Your assessment of the adequacy of this profit will depend on a number of factors including any other opportunities that are available to you, the level of risk that you are taking, etc.

This exercise demonstrates that breakeven analysis can help you to make better-informed business decisions, but the analysis itself will not produce a definitive answer as to whether this is a worthwhile proposition. Your own management judgement is still required.

10.3.3 Graphical breakeven analysis

The example that we have just worked through can be depicted graphically in a breakeven chart as shown in Figure 10.6.

- The fixed cost line is drawn as £5,015 per month
- The total cost line is then superimposed on this. It joins the total cost at zero activity (i.e. the fixed cost of £5,015) to the total cost of £8,215 at the forecast activity of 400 customers per month.

Variable cost = 400 x £8	£3,200
Fixed cost	£5,015
Total cost	£8,215

- The sales line joins the origin (zero customers = zero revenue) to the total sales revenue at the forecast activity of 400 customers, i.e. 400 x £25 = £10,000 per month.

Figure 10.6: Breakeven chart for restaurant business

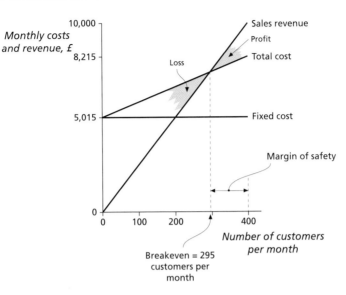

The point where the sales revenue line cuts the total cost line is the breakeven point, i.e. 295 customers per month, as we have already calculated. The areas of profit and loss can also be identified, and the margin of safety can be read off as the difference between the forecast number of customers and the breakeven point.

A breakeven chart like this one can often be helpful in assisting less numerate managers to appreciate the significance of the cost behaviour patterns, the size of the margin of safety, and so on.

10.3.4 Breakeven analysis: another example

LearnFast is a driving school which employs a number of part-time driving instructors and leases a fleet of vehicles. The driving instructors are paid an hourly rate and they work flexible hours which depend on the demand for their services. At present the school's pupils pay £20 per one hour lesson and LearnFast's cost structure is as follows:

Variable cost per lesson   £15
Fixed cost per month   £20,000

Current sales are 12,000 lessons per month.

Exercise
What costs might be variable for this driving school, and what costs might be fixed?

Solution

For variable costs you might have thought of fuel and instructors' wages. This sort of cost would increase with the number of lessons sold and in this example they amount to £15 per lesson. Fixed costs would include administrative salaries, car lease payments and the rent on the office premises. These costs would not increase with the number of lessons sold (within a reasonable range) and in this example they amount to £20,000 per month.

Exercise

Calculate LearnFast's breakeven point, the margin of safety and the monthly profit.

Solution

Contribution per lesson = selling price less variable cost

£20 – £15 = £5 per lesson

This contribution goes towards paying the monthly fixed costs. When the fixed costs are just covered, breakeven point will have been reached. Breakeven point is therefore monthly fixed costs divided by contribution per lesson:

$$\text{Breakeven point} = \frac{£20,000}{£5} = \qquad 4,000 \ \text{lessons}$$

Actual sales =	12,000 lessons
Therefore, margin of safety =	8,000 lessons
Each lesson earns a contribution of	£5 (multiply)
Therefore, monthly profit =	£40,000

The managing director has suggested that, since there is little opportunity to increase sales, LearnFast should upgrade their fleet of vehicles. Fuel consumption would be lower with the new vehicles and market research suggests that pupils would be prepared to pay £22 per lesson for the improved dual-control facilities.

With the new fleet, LearnFast's cost structure would be as follows:

Variable cost per lesson	£14
Fixed cost per month	£40,000

It is not anticipated that sales can be increased above the current level of 12,000 lessons per month.

Notice that the variable cost of each hour's lesson is reduced to £14: the result of the improved fuel consumption. However, the fixed cost has doubled to £40,000 per month: the increased car lease payments.

Exercise

Calculate the breakeven point, the margin of safety and the monthly profit after the managing director's proposed changes. Comment on whether or not you think these proposals should be adopted.

Solution

Contribution per lesson (£22 – £14)	£8 per lesson
Breakeven point ($^{£40,000}/_{£8}$)	5,000 lessons
Actual sales	12,000 lessons
Margin of safety	7,000 lessons
Contribution per lesson	£8 (multiply)
Monthly profit	£56,000

Summary of results:

	Present situation	Proposed situation
Breakeven point	4,000 lessons	5,000 lessons
Margin of safety	8,000 lessons	7,000 lessons
Monthly profit	£40,000	£56,000

The forecast 40 per cent increase in profit is certainly attractive but the decision to adopt the proposals would depend on a number of factors including:

- What is LearnFast's attitude to risk? The breakeven point is higher and the margin of safety is smaller. This means that the business as a whole will be more risky.
- The market appears to be stagnant: the managing director has stated that there is little opportunity to increase sales. This means that competitors will be fighting hard to attract LearnFast's customers, since this will be the only way that companies can grow. Every lesson that LearnFast loses to competitors in the future will reduce overall contribution by £8. In the present situation, each lesson lost reduces contribution by only £5. This again reflects the more risky situation with the new proposals.
- On the other hand, the improved contribution per lesson means that, if LearnFast could increase sales in the future, contribution and profits would grow at a much faster rate.
- How reliable is the market research that indicates that customers would be prepared to pay a higher rate for lessons in the improved vehicles? If the research predictions are incorrect, LearnFast could find themselves committed to a higher level of fixed costs but unable to increase the selling price in the way that they had hoped.

This exercise should have demonstrated once again how management accounting information can help managers to make better-informed decisions, but it cannot provide a definitive answer as to whether or not a particular proposal is acceptable.

10.3.5 Operational gearing

Operational gearing is a term used to describe the relationship of the fixed cost to the total cost of an organisation. It is similar to financial gearing that you learned about in Chapter 7.

Higher operational gearing means that, as sales increase, profits increase at a faster rate; vice versa if sales fall. In the last exercise, LearnFast was considering a change to its cost structure that would increase its operational gearing. The monthly fixed cost was expected to double and the unit variable cost was expected to reduce.

Exercise

Calculate LearnFast's monthly profits from sales of 14,400 lessons

(a) in the present situation

(b) after the managing director's proposed changes

Solution

	Present situation	Proposed situation
Contribution per lesson	£5	£8
Contribution from 14,400 lessons	£72,000	£115,200
Fixed costs	£20,000	£40,000
Monthly profit	£52,000	£75,200

This exercise demonstrates that, with a 20 per cent increase in sales (14,400 lessons compared with 12,000 lessons), the monthly profit increases by:

	Present situation	Proposed situation
£40,000 profit increased to £52,000	30% increase	
£56,000 profit increased to £75,200		34% increase

In both situations the profit increased by more than 20 per cent because of the gearing effect of the spreading of fixed costs.

However, with the proposed situation the percentage increase in profit was higher because of the higher level of operational gearing.

Experiment for yourself, by reducing the volume of sales by 20 per cent, to prove that the percentage fall in profit will be greater in the proposed situation.

Higher operational gearing can therefore be advantageous if sales activity is expected to increase in the future. However, management need to be aware that profit levels would fall more rapidly if activity levels began to decrease.

10.3.6 The limitations of CVP analysis

The examples in this section of the chapter have shown that CVP analysis can be a useful tool to investigate the relationship between an organisation's costs and revenues. However, it does have its limitations in terms of practical applicability. These limitations stem mostly from the assumptions which underlie the analysis:

(a) Costs are assumed to behave in a linear fashion. Unit variable costs are assumed to remain constant and fixed costs are assumed to be unaffected by changes in activity levels. Breakeven charts can in fact be adjusted to cope with non-linear variable costs or steps in fixed costs but too many changes in behaviour patterns can make the charts very cluttered and difficult to use.
(b) Sales revenues are assumed to be constant for each unit sold. This may be unrealistic because of the necessity to reduce the selling price to achieve higher sales volumes.
(c) It is assumed that activity is the only factor affecting costs and revenues. Other factors such as inflation and technology changes are ignored. This is one of the reasons why CVP analysis is limited to being essentially a short-term decision aid.

However, much CVP analysis is carried out as the basis for forecasting future outcomes. Since a lot of the forecast data will be subject to inaccuracies, these simplifying assumptions may not lead to significant further error.

10.4 Marginal analysis

In the remainder of this chapter we will be looking at a number of common decision-making situations and seeing how a choice may be made between alternative courses of action.

Generally, if alternatives are being compared there is little point in including data which is common to all courses of action. Management attention should be focused on those costs and revenues which will alter as a result of the decision. In other words, the incremental costs and revenues should be highlighted. In many cases the fixed costs will not be altered by a decision and they will not be relevant – they are not *incremental* costs and should be excluded from the analysis. However, in some situations there may be a step in the fixed cost and this extra, or incremental, fixed cost should be taken into the analysis.

We will now work through a number of examples to demonstrate how this might be done.

10.4.1 Utilising spare capacity: example

The Perfect Plastics Company (PP) manufactures packs of plastic food containers for use in domestic freezers. They sell them to supermarket chains and to department stores, under the brand name 'Freezit'.

Sales volume is currently 80,000 packs per period, but the company has the capacity to manufacture a further 20,000 packs per period. Despite repeated attempts to seek new customers, PP's sales force has not succeeded in increasing sales above the current 80,000 packs per period.

An outline profit statement for PP's current situation is as follows:

Current profit per period

	£	£
Sales value		800,000
Variable costs	320,000	
Fixed costs	380,000	
		700,000
Profit		100,000

A large supermarket chain has recently approached PP to ask them to manufacture packs on an 'own-label' basis, i.e. the packs would be labelled with the supermarket's own brand name. They would be willing to purchase 20,000 packs per period but they are only prepared to pay 50 per cent of the normal selling price.

Unit variable costs would not be altered by the proposal but fixed costs would increase by £4,000 per period, because extra employees would be needed to help with the packing.

Is this a worthwhile proposal from a financial point of view?
We need to determine the incremental costs and incremental revenues that will arise from this proposal.

Current selling price per pack: $£800,000/80,000 = £10$
$\therefore$ Proposed selling price $= 50\% \times £10 = £5$
Variable cost per pack $= £320,000/80,000 = £4$

An outline profit statement can now be prepared for the proposal.

	£	£
Incremental revenue 20,000 x £5		100,000
Variable costs 20,000 x £4	80,000	
Incremental fixed costs	4,000	
		84,000
Incremental profit		16,000

The proposal generates an incremental profit of £16,000 and is therefore worthwhile from a financial point of view

Exercise
1. How many packs must the supermarket chain purchase each period if PP is to break even on the proposal?
2. What other factors should PP consider before making a decision?

Solution
1. Contribution per 'own-label' pack:
   Selling price £5 – variable cost £4 = £1

   Breakeven number of packs is the incremental fixed costs divided by the contribution per pack:
   $$£4,000/£1 = 4,000 \text{ packs}$$

   The purchase of 4,000 packs will generate a contribution of £4,000 to exactly cover the incremental fixed costs.

2. The sort of factors that you might have suggested include:

   - Does the supermarket chain guarantee to take 20,000 packs per period? If they did not take any packs in a particular period, then profits would fall by £4,000 because of the extra wage payments.
   - Would this contract affect PP's full-price business?
     - would other customers also demand the lower price?
     - would the supermarket's customers buy the own-brand pack instead of the higher-priced 'Freezit' pack?
   - Would the unit variable costs definitely be the same? What about any extra distribution and storage costs?
   - With a unit contribution of only £1, there is not much room to accommodate any cost increases. Is the contract price fixed in the long term, or can price increases be negotiated in the future?

- Is there no likelihood of an increase in the full-price business in future? Tying up 20 per cent of capacity for low-price business could be damaging to future expansion plans.
- Can the excess capacity be sold or rented to a third party?
  The potential saving in fixed costs may be higher than the £16,000 profit generated by this proposal.

10.4.2 Closing a department: example

Feminine Fashions (FF) is a retail ladies' clothes shop which has three departments that operate from the same premises. The results for the latest period are as follows:

	Clothes and coats £000	Nightwear and lingerie £000	Boots and shoes £000	Total £000
Sales revenue	78	120	21	219
Variable costs	48	68	16	132
Contribution	30	52	5	87
Fixed costs	23	34	9	66
Profit/(loss)	7	18	(4)	21

FF's directors are considering closing the boots and shoes department, because it makes a loss.

However, if we assume that fixed costs would be incurred even if boots and shoes were discontinued, FF's profit would fall to £16,000 per period if the boots and shoes department was closed:

	Clothes and coats £000	Nightwear and lingerie £000	Total £000
Sales revenue	78	120	198
Variable costs	48	68	116
Contribution	30	52	82
Fixed costs			66
Profit			16

The £5,000 contribution from the boots and shoes department would be lost, therefore this department should not be closed unless a more profitable use can be found for the space that it occupies.

Exercise

Would your advice be altered if, as a result of the closure of the boots and shoes department, staff salaries of £2,000 per period could be saved and sales of clothes and coats could be increased by 20 per cent? Produce a revised profit statement to show this situation.

Solution

Remember that the variable costs would also increase by 20 per cent.

Revised profit statement

	Clothes and coats £000	Nightwear and lingerie £000	Total £000
Sales revenue (78 x 1.2)	93.6	120	213.6
Variable costs (48 x 1.2)	57.6	68	125.6
Contribution	36.0	52	88.0
Fixed costs (66 – 2)			64.0
Profit			24.0

Profit would increase to £24,000 per period therefore this is a worthwhile proposal.

This type of analysis can also be used in product range decisions, i.e. when managers are considering discontinuing a product or service because it appears to be loss making. The key performance measure must be the product's contribution, less any attributable fixed costs, which in FF's case were fixed salaries of £2,000 that could be saved by the department's closure.

Attributable fixed costs are those which can be identified specifically with a product or service and which would be saved if that product or service was discontinued.

However, before we leave this example it is worth stressing again the importance of considering non-financial factors in the decision. One of the most important factors to consider in a product/service range decision, or in deciding to close a department, is the possible interdependence of the products or departments.

For example, in FF's case it might be worth keeping the boots and shoes department even if it does not generate a contribution. Customers may be attracted into the shop by the boots and shoes department and may then also buy articles from the other departments.

Likewise in a multi-product firm, if one product was discontinued customers may go elsewhere for all their requirements, because they expect a single supplier to provide a full range of related products.

10.4.3 Make or buy decisions

Managers will sometimes be faced with the decision of whether to produce internally a product or service which they sell, or to buy it from an external supplier. For example, a manufacturer of washing machines may decide to subcontract part of their product range to an external manufacturer, perhaps because they have insufficient capacity or because the supplier is able to supply the washing machines cheaper than they can be produced internally.

Alternatively, the washing machine manufacturer may decide to subcontract only a part of the manufacturing process. For example, they may purchase certain components ready-made from external suppliers, but manufacture internally the remainder of their requirements.

However, make or buy decisions do not apply only to manufacturing concerns. A service organisation might also subcontract part of its services. For example, a delivery firm might subcontract overseas delivery to a company which is based in the relevant country. Furthermore, any organisation might decide to subcontract a part of its operations which is currently being performed internally. For example, the organisation's data processing or canteen operations may be subcontracted to an external specialist company.

Exercise

Multi-products (MP) Limited uses component P in its main product. It currently manufactures its own requirements of component P but an external supplier has offered to supply all its requirements for a price of £36 each.

The cost of manufacturing component P internally is £42 as follows:

	£ per unit
Direct material	11
Direct labour	16
Variable overhead	4
Fixed overhead	11
	42

The supplier's price is lower than the internal cost of manufacture, so on purely financial grounds, should the component be purchased externally or manufactured internally? What assumptions do you need to make in order to reach a decision?

Solution

The following assumptions will be made:

- Fixed overheads would be incurred even if the component was not manu-factured internally
- None of the resources used in internal manufacture are in short supply

The costs which would be saved by purchasing externally are the variable costs only:

	£ per unit
Direct material	11
Direct labour	16
Variable overhead	4
	31

The cost is lower than the external supplier's price, therefore MP should con-tinue to manufacture its own requirements.

10.4.4 Opportunity costs

The Chartered Institute of Management Accountants (CIMA) defines an opportunity cost in its *Official Terminology* as follows:

'The value of the benefit sacrificed when one course of action is chosen, in preference to an alternative. The opportunity cost is represented by the forgone potential benefit from the best rejected course of action.'

An opportunity cost can be demonstrated by extending the example of MP Limited from the previous exercise.

The manufacture of component P uses specialist labour skills and it is not possible to recruit any more suitably skilled employees. If the component was not manufactured internally, it would be possible to use the available spe-cialist labour to manufacture product M.

Product M sells for £19 per unit and incurs variable cost of £14 per unit as follows:

	£ per unit
Direct material	5
Direct labour	8
Variable overhead	1
Total variable cost	14

All the labour input consists of the specially skilled employees, who are paid at the rate of £8 per hour.

We will now see whether these circumstances would alter our advice to manufacture component P internally.

Product M generates a contribution of £5 per unit (£19 – £14) and takes one hour to manufacture (£8 direct labour ÷ £8 per hour).

Each unit of component P takes two hours (£16 direct labour ÷ £8 per hour).

Every time a component P is manufactured the company loses the opportunity to manufacture two units of M, which would each earn £5 contribution. The costs of internal manufacture of P can therefore be revised as follows.

	£ per unit
Variable cost (as before)	31
Opportunity cost: contribution forgone (2 x £5)	10
	41

This cost is higher than the external supplier's price of £36, therefore in this situation the component should be purchased externally.

You will meet opportunity costs again in the next section of this chapter, in the context of relevant costs.

Exercise
What other factors should be considered before making the recommendation to purchase component P externally?

Solution
Other factors which you might have considered include the following:

- The quality and reliability of the external supply
- The possibility of seeking external sources of supply for product M
- The ability to train or recruit more personnel with suitable skills

10.5 Relevant costs

Relevant costs are those which will be affected by the decision being taken. All relevant costs should be considered in management decision-making. If a cost will remain unaltered regardless of the decision being taken then it is called a non-relevant cost.

10.5.1 Non-relevant costs

Costs which are not usually relevant in management decisions include the following:

(a) **Sunk or past costs**, which is money already spent which cannot now be recovered. An example of a sunk cost is expenditure which has been incurred in developing a new product. The money cannot now be recovered even if a decision is taken to abandon further development of the new product. The cost is therefore not relevant to future decisions concerning the product.

(b) **Absorbed fixed overheads** which will not increase or decrease as a result of the decision being taken. We saw an example of this when we were looking at the decision criteria for deciding whether to close a department in a retail shop.

(c) **Expenditure which will be incurred in the future, but as a result of decisions taken in the past** which cannot now be changed. This can sometimes cause confusion because it is a future cost. However, it will be incurred regardless of the decision being taken and therefore it is not relevant. An example of this type of cost could be expenditure on special packaging for a new product, where the packaging has been ordered and delivered but not yet paid for. The company is obliged to pay for the packaging even if they decide not to proceed with the product, therefore even though it is a future cash flow it is not a relevant cost of the decision to proceed.

(d) **Historical cost depreciation**. Depreciation calculations do not result in any future cash flows. They are merely the bookkeeping entries which are designed to spread the original cost of an asset over its useful life. For example, in the case of MP Limited deciding to subcontract the manufacture of component P, a manager might state: 'I disagree. Internal manufacture must be continued because we have a special machine which we purchased specifically to manufacture component P. The machine cannot be sold or used for another purpose and there is still £30,000 of the net book value to be written off'. The future cash flows of MP Limited will not be affected by the decision to discontinue the use of the machine therefore the £30,000 net book value is not relevant.

Now you should have a good idea of how to identify relevant and non-relevant costs, so attempt the following exercise to test your understanding.

Exercise

Flexible Training (FT) Limited provides specialist in-company training courses. The company has been in negotiation for a number of months with AB Limited, attempting to secure a contract for a one-day in-company seminar. AB Limited is known to have asked other suppliers for quotations and is now requesting a final price from all potential suppliers.

It is vital that FT should secure this particular contract, as it is likely to lead to a great deal of profitable business once the quality of the course has been experienced.

You are asked to state the relevant cost of the decision to proceed and bid for the contract.

The following information may be relevant:

1. £200 has been paid already to the presenter to develop the course.

2. Fees and expenses of £450 will be paid to the presenter if the course goes ahead.

3. A video tape will be hired for the course at a cost of £80 for the day.

4. Another video tape has been purchased for £500, specifically for this course. The supplier has stated that £350 can be refunded for the tape, but only if it is returned unopened.

5. Printing of the course papers will cost £145. This consists of £110 for the incremental variable costs of printing (paper, ink and power, etc.) and £35 of apportioned fixed costs of the internal printing department.

6. Other costs to be incurred directly as a result of this contract are £120.

7. FT's policy is to add 50 per cent to the cost of each contract in order to recover the company's general fixed overheads. It is not expected that general overheads will increase as a result of this contract.

Solution

The relevant costs are those which will be incurred in the future as a result of a decision to proceed and place a final bid for the contract.

Relevant cost (see explanatory notes)

Item no.	£
1	–
2	450
3	80
4	350
5	110
6	120
7	–
Total relevant cost	1,110

Notes

1.	This is a sunk or past cost.
2 & 3.	These are relevant costs of the decision to proceed with a bid.
4.	This is the opportunity cost of using the tape for the course. The original cost of the tape (£500) is sunk and not relevant to the future. If the company sends the tape back now, it can recover £350. If it uses the tape for the course it will lose the opportunity to recover this £350, therefore this is the cost of the decision to proceed. It might be argued that this cost could be spread over a number of potential presentations of the course. However, this is anticipating something which may not occur.
5.	Only the incremental variable costs are relevant. The fixed costs would be incurred anyway.
6.	These are incremental costs which are relevant.
7.	These overheads will not increase as a result of the contract therefore a general absorption charge is not a relevant cost.

10.5.2 Minimum price quotations for special orders

This exercise determined the relevant cost of the important contract. This cost represents the minimum price which the company could afford to quote if they wish to make neither a profit nor a loss on the contract. As long as the customer pays £1,110 for the contract, FT's profits will not be affected.

Obviously this represents the absolute minimum price that could be charged. It is unlikely that FT would actually charge this amount. They would probably wish to add a profit margin to improve the company's profits.

However, this absolute minimum price does give managers a starting point for their pricing decision. They know that the company will be worse off if the price is less than £1,110. AB Limited may try to obtain some information concerning the likely prices to be tendered by their competitors. If their prices are likely to be less than or close to £1,110 then AB knows that they will not be able to offer a competitive price. On the other hand, if competitors are likely to tender a much higher price then the managers know that they are able to price competitively.

10.6 Summary

1. Cost behaviour patterns depict the way that costs behave in relation to the level of activity.
2. An understanding of cost behaviour patterns is necessary in order to perform cost-volume-profit analysis.
3. The margin of safety is the difference between the breakeven point and the projected level of activity.
4. Operational gearing is a term used to describe the relationship of the fixed cost to the total cost of an organisation.
5. Marginal analysis involves identifying and focusing on only those costs and revenues which will change as a result of the decision being taken.
6. An attributable fixed cost is one which can be identified with a particular item or activity.
7. Relevant costs are those which will be affected by the decision being taken.

Review questions
1. Sketch a graph of the total fixed cost and the fixed cost per unit. (sections 10.2.1, 10.2.2)
2. How is the breakeven point calculated? (section 10.3.1)
3. What is meant by high operational gearing? (section 10.3.5)
4. What are the limitations of CVP analysis? (section 10.3.6)
5. What is an opportunity cost? (section 10.4.4)

Self-test questions

? 1. A company manufactures a single product, C. Unit cost and selling price
   information for product C is as follows.

	£ per unit
Direct material and labour	13
Variable overhead	3
Fixed overhead	4
	20
Profit	8
Selling price	28

Budgeted output and sales of product C amount to 6,000 units per month.

Required
Calculate the following:

(a) The monthly breakeven point, in units
(b) The monthly margin of safety
(c) The monthly profit

? 2. An engineering company has been offered the opportunity to bid for a
   contract which requires a special component. Currently, the company has
   a component in stock, which has a net book value of £250. This component could be used in the contract, but would require modification at a
   cost of £50. There is no other foreseeable use for the component held in
   stock. Alternatively, the company could purchase a new specialist component for £280.

   What is the relevant cost of the component required for this contract?

? 3. BSE Veterinary Services is a specialist laboratory carrying out tests on cattle
   to ascertain whether the cattle have any infection. At present, the laboratory carries out 12,000 tests each period but, because of current difficulties with the beef herd, demand is expected to increase to 18,000 tests
   a period, which would require an additional shift to be worked.
   The current cost of carrying out a full test is:

	£ per test
Materials	115
Technicians' wages	30
Variable overhead	12
Fixed overhead	50

Working the additional shift would:

(i) Require a shift premium of 50 per cent to be paid to the technicians on the additional shift;

(ii) Enable a quantity discount of 20 per cent to be obtained for all materials if an order was placed to cover 18,000 tests;

(iii) Increase fixed costs by £700,000 per period.

The current fee per test is £300.

Requirements

(a) Prepare a profit statement for the current 12,000 test capacity.

(b) Prepare a profit statement if the additional shift was worked and 18,000 tests were carried out.

(c) Comment on three other factors which should be considered before any decision is taken.

Answers to self-test questions

1. (a) Fixed overhead per month = 6,000 units x £4 = £24,000

$$\text{Monthly breakeven point} = \frac{\text{fixed overhead}}{\text{contribution per unit}} = \frac{£24,000}{£(28\text{-}13\text{-}3)} = 2000 \text{ units}$$

(b) Margin of safety = budgeted sales - breakeven sales

= (6,000 - 2,000) units

= 4,000 units, or 67% of budgeted sales

(c) Monthly profit = margin of safety units x contribution per unit

= 4,000 units x £12 = £48,000

2. The net book value is not relevant; it is a sunk or past cost. The company would not purchase a new component because it would be cheaper to modify the existing component in stock, incurring an incremental cost of £50.

3. (a) **Profit statement for 12,000 tests**

	£ per test	£000	£000
Sales revenue	300		3,600
Materials	115	1,380	
Technicians' wages	30	360	
Variable overhead	12	144	
			1,884
Contribution			1,716
Fixed overhead	50		600
Profit			1,116

(b) **Profit statement for 18,000 tests**

	No of tests	£ per test	£000	£000
Sales revenue	18,000	300		5,400
Materials (note 1)	18,000	92	1,656	
Technicians' wages (note 2)	12,000	30	360	
	6,000	45	270	
Variable overhead	18,000	12	216	
				2,502
Contribution				2,898
Fixed costs (note 3)				1,300
Profit				1,598

Notes

1. Material cost per test	=	£115 x 80% = £92
2. Wages cost per test for second shift	=	£30 x 150% = £45
3. Fixed costs for 12,000 test capacity	=	£600,000
Increase for extra 6,000 tests	=	£700,000
Fixed costs for 18,000 test capacity	=	£1,300,000

(c) Other factors to consider include the following.
   (i) If the increased demand will continue for the foreseeable future it may be worth while taking on more technicians so that the extra shift, and the consequent shift premium, are not necessary.
   (ii) Will the accuracy of the tests be affected by requiring the technicians to work an additional shift?
   (iii) Have all costs been considered? For example will it be necessary to rent additional storage space for the extra materials to be purchased?
   (iv) Instead of accommodating the increased demand, it may be possible to earn more profit by increasing the selling price, to reduce the rise in demand.

Budgetary planning and control

11.1 Introduction

In this chapter you will be learning about budgets: what they are and how they are prepared and used. You will also be introduced to the importance of communication in the budgetary planning process, and the human aspects of budgeting.

11.2 The purposes of budgeting

Suppose that you and three of your friends decide to start a small business. You will be buying and selling quality handmade crafts, gifts and greetings cards, starting initially in a medium-sized high street shop. You will be the financial manager and your friends will take on the following roles:

- Chris: purchasing manager
- Sandy: shop manager
- Frankie: marketing and publicity manager

You have arranged a business bank account and each of you has paid in their savings to give the business a healthy initial cash balance. So now you need to start running the business.

Chris seeks out suitable suppliers and begins to place orders for stock. Sandy employs a part-time sales assistant and orders some fittings for the shop. Frankie places advertisements in the local paper and orders 100 helium balloons ready for the Grand Opening.

You write out the cheques for all these expenses and carefully record the transactions on your newly purchased computerised bookkeeping system. No problem so far: you have a healthy starting cash balance. Soon the customers start to arrive and you pay the cash receipts into the bank, carefully recording the receipts on the system. Then things start to go wrong. Customers are flocking to your shop and sales are soaring. You are probably thinking, 'surely things are going right if business is booming?' But look at what is happening:

- Sandy has decided to take on two more staff – more help is needed to manage the bulging stock room and deal with the flow of customers. Sandy has also agreed to pay regular overtime to two staff members who stay late to sort out the shop displays ready for the next day.
- Chris has agreed to pay premium rates to a supplier who guarantees next-day delivery. He argues that a new business cannot afford to turn away enthusiastic customers because of a lack of stock.
- Frankie has ordered 5,000 glossy leaflets and is recruiting a small team of temporary staff to deliver the leaflets to local houses – the idea is to reinforce the tremendous word-of-mouth praise that is spreading around the neighbourhood.

Everybody is caught up in the euphoria of booming sales and they are probably spending all of the money that is being received from customers, and more besides. Your healthy cash balance will not last long at this rate!

So how can this situation be avoided?

The answer is by using budgets. Budgets are monetary plans prepared in advance for the forthcoming period. They detail the amount of expenditure that each budget holder is authorised to incur or the income that they are expected to generate.

Each of the four people in your business would be a budget holder.

The actual income or expenditure can be compared with these budgets as the period progresses so that budget holders can tell whether their part of the business is proceeding according to budget. If it is not then they can take action to correct the deviation from plan, or they may need to get together to prepare another budget if the original is no longer representative of the current situation.

In our example, the four managers would need to get together to produce another budget once it became obvious that revenue was exceeding expectations and that the original plans for expenditure and revenue would have to be revised.

Our business consisted of just four people, yet it was still difficult to coordinate their activities without a formalised plan or budget. Imagine what it would be like in a large organisation with dozens or hundreds of managers, each incurring expenditure or generating revenue, if there was no formalised budgetary plan to coordinate their activities.

Budgets, therefore, have two main roles.

- They act as authorities to spend or as targets to achieve, i.e. they give authority to budget managers to incur expenditure in their part of the organisation or they provide targets for the revenue-generating parts of the organisation.
- They act as comparators for current performance, by providing a yard-stick against which current activities can be monitored.

These two roles are combined in a system of budgetary planning and control.

11.2.1 Budgetary planning and control

Planning the activities of an organisation ensures that the organisation sets out in the right direction. Individuals in the organisation will have definite targets which they will aim to achieve. Without a formalised plan the organisation will lack direction and managers will not be aware of their own targets and responsibilities. Neither will they appreciate how their activities relate to those of other managers within the organisation.

A formalised plan will help to ensure a coordinated approach and the planning process itself will force managers to continually think ahead, planning and reviewing their activities in advance.

However, the budgetary process should not stop with the plan. The organisation has started out in the right direction but to ensure that it continues on course it is management's responsibility to exercise control.

Control is best achieved by comparison of the actual results with the original plan. Appropriate action can then be taken to correct any deviations from the plan.

The two activities of planning and control must go hand in hand. Carrying out the budgetary planning exercise without using the plan for control purposes is performing only part of the task.

 Comparison of actual results with a budgetary plan, and taking action to correct deviations, is known as feedback control.

11.2.2 What is a budget?

A budget could be defined as 'a quantified plan of action relating to a given period of time'.

For a budget to be useful it must be quantified. For example, it would not be particularly useful for the purposes of planning and control if a budget was set as follows:

'We plan to spend as little as possible in running the printing department this year'; or 'We plan to produce as many units as we can possibly sell this quarter.'

These are merely vague indicators of general direction; they are not quantified plans. They will not provide much assistance in management's task of planning and controlling the organisation.

These 'budgets' could perhaps be modified as follows:

'Budgeted revenue expenditure for the printing department this year is £60,000'; and 'Budgeted production for the quarter is 4,700 units'.

The quantification of the budgets has provided:

- A definite target for planning purposes; and
- A yardstick for control purposes.

11.2.3 The budget period

You may have noticed that in each of these 'budgets' the time period was different. The first budget was prepared for a year and the second was for a quarter. The time period for which a budget is prepared and used is called the budget period. It can be any length to suit management purposes but it is usually one year.

The length chosen for the budget period will depend on many factors, including the nature of the organisation and the type of expenditure being considered. Each budget period can be subdivided into control periods, also of varying lengths, depending on the level of control which management wishes to exercise. The usual length of a control period is one month, which means that control reports for comparison of actual results with the budget will be prepared monthly.

11.2.4 Objectives, long-term plans and budgetary plans

The first stage in planning the activities of an organisation is to set its overall objectives or mission. This is what the organisation is aiming to achieve in the long run. The most common objective of profit-making organisations is the maximisation of the organisation's wealth, but there could also be other objectives such as survival, expansion, and long-term stability.

The long-term plan details how these objectives will be achieved, covering a period of, say, five years. The long-term plan would cover in broad terms aspects such as the following:

- Which products or services the business will offer to customers
- Which markets the business will operate in
- Whether growth will be achieved by internal growth or by acquiring other businesses
- The resources required, in terms of finance, personnel, equipment, etc.

Figure 11.1: Objectives, long-term plans and budgetary plans

The annual budget would then be set within the framework of the long-term plan (see Figure 11.1). An organisation's annual budget is an interim step towards the achievement of the long-term plan, providing more detail in terms of sales revenues, revenue expenditure and capital expenditure, etc.

 The short term for one organisation may be the medium or long term for another, depending on the type of activity in which the organisation is involved.

11.3 The preparation of budgets

The process of preparing and using budgets will differ from one organisation to another. However, there are a number of key requirements in the design of a budgetary planning and control process.

11.3.1 Co-ordination: the budget committee

The need for co-ordination in the planning process is paramount. The inter-relationship among the functional budgets was demonstrated in our example at the beginning of this chapter. Frankie's activities as marketing manager affected how busy Sandy, the shop manager and Chris, the purchasing manager, would be. Chris's activities in purchasing stock affected Sandy's need for staff to receive, check and store the stock. All their activities affected you as the financial manager, for example in paying the invoices for their purchases and ensuring that the cash resources were available for the expenses that they incurred.

This means that one budget cannot be prepared in isolation, without reference to several others. The best way to achieve the necessary coordination is to set up a budget committee. In our example the four managers would comprise the necessary committee. However, in a larger organisation there should be a representative on the committee from each part of the organisation. There would be representatives from sales, marketing, personnel, and so on.

The budget committee should meet regularly to review the progress of the budgetary planning process and to resolve any problems that have arisen. These meetings will effectively bring together the whole organisation in one room, to ensure that a coordinated approach is adopted in budget preparation.

11.3.2 Information: the budget manual

Effective budgetary planning and control relies on the provision of adequate information to the individuals involved in the planning process. Many of these information needs are contained in the budget manual. This is a collection of documents which contains key information for those involved in the planning process.

Typical contents could include the following:

(a) An introductory explanation of the budgetary planning and control process. Participants should be made aware of the advantage to them and to the organisation of an efficient planning and control process. This introduction should give participants an understanding of the workings of the planning process, and of the sort of information that they can expect to receive as part of the control process.

(b) A form of organisation chart to show who is responsible for the preparation of each functional budget and the way in which budgets are interrelated.

(c) A timetable for the preparation of each budget. This will prevent the formation of a 'bottleneck' with the late preparation of one budget holding up the preparation of all others.

(d) Copies of all forms to be completed by those responsible for preparing budgets, with explanations concerning their completion.

(e) A list of the organisation's account codes with full explanations of how to use them.

(f) Information concerning key assumptions to be made by managers in their budgets, to ensure consistency throughout the organisation, for example the rate of inflation, key exchange rates, etc.

(g) The name and location of the person to be contacted concerning any problems encountered in preparing the budgetary plans. This will usually be the coordinator of the budget committee (the budget officer) and will probably be a senior accountant.

11.3.3 Early identification of the principal budget factor

The principal budget factor is the factor which limits the activities of the organisation. The early identification of this factor is important in the budgetary planning process because it indicates which budget should be prepared first.

For example, if sales volume is the principal budget factor then the sales budget must be prepared first, based on the available sales forecasts. All other budgets should then be linked to this.

Alternatively, machine capacity may be limited for the forthcoming period and therefore machine capacity is the principal budget factor. In this case the production budget must be prepared first and all other budgets must be linked to this.

Failure to identify the principal budget factor at an early stage could lead to delays later on when managers realise that the targets they have been working on are not feasible (see Figure 11.2).

11.3.4 The master budget: the iterative process of budgetary planning

The master budget is a summary of all the functional budgets. It may include a budgeted profit and loss account (or income and expenditure account) a cash-flow budget and a budgeted balance sheet. It is this master budget which is submitted to senior managers for approval because they should not be burdened with an excessive amount of detail. The master budget is designed to give the summarised information that they need to determine whether the budget is an acceptable plan for the forthcoming period.

The criteria used to assess the suitability of budgets may include adherence to the organisation's long-term objectives, profitability, liquidity, and so on. The senior managers may require amendments to be made or they may wish to see the effect of changes in key decision variables. The budget will then be returned to the budget committee and budget managers will be asked to revise their budgets and resubmit them to form a new master budget. This will be presented once more to the senior management team until a cohesive plan is agreed and accepted as the organisation's target for the year.

187

Figure 11.2: Summary of the steps in the budgetary planning process

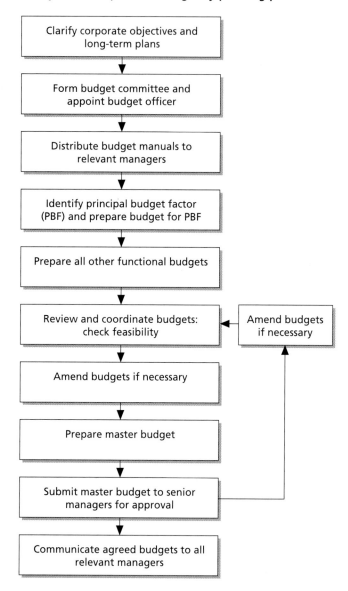

This process can involve several iterations, which have been made easier with the development of computer programs such as spreadsheets, etc., which help to refine the budgetary planning process.

11.4 Incremental and zero-based budgeting

In the example which we reviewed at the beginning of this chapter it was relatively straightforward to see how, once we have forecast the sales volume for the craft shop, many of the other budgets could be prepared using this as a basis.

Chris's purchasing budget would be based on the sales budget, with any adjustments necessary to allow for proposed increases or decreases in stock. Sandy's shop staff budget would also be based on the sales budget, and on Chris's plans for stockholding. But what about the budget for marketing expenditure, where outputs are not so clearly linked to inputs? And how would you prepare budgets for costs such as training, and research into new product lines? Determining the level of expenditure to be included in this type of budget is not quite so straightforward.

This type of cost is called a discretionary cost, also known as policy or managed costs.

11.4.1 Incremental budgeting

Many budgets are set using an incremental approach. This means that the budget for each period is determined by reference to what was spent last period plus, perhaps, an allowance for anticipated inflation.

Exercise
Can you identify any problems with using this incremental approach to budgeting?

Solution
- This approach is unlikely to result in the optimum allocation of resources.
- It tends to perpetuate inefficient and unnecessary practices and there is no incentive for managers to consider new ways of achieving the objectives for their part of the organisation.
- There may be an incentive to overspend if managers know that their budget allowance for the forthcoming period will be based on their expenditure during this period.

11.4.2 Zero-based budgeting

Zero-based budgeting (ZBB) was developed as an alternative to the incremental approach. It is so called because it requires each budget to be prepared and justified from zero, instead of simply using last period's budget or actual expenditure as a base. Incremental levels of expenditure on each activity are evaluated according to the resulting incremental benefits. Available resources are then allocated where they can be used most effectively.

The major advantage of ZBB exercises is that managers are forced to consider alternative ways of achieving the objectives for their activity and they are required to justify the activities which they currently undertake.

Exercise
Can you identify any problems with using a zero-based approach to budgeting?

Solution
- ZBB exercises can be very time consuming.
- It can be difficult to identify the anticipated incremental benefit to result from incremental amounts of expenditure.
- Managers may feel threatened if their area of the business is subject to the level of scrutiny inherent in a ZBB exercise.

The time-consuming nature of ZBB exercises means that many organisations perform a zero-based analysis on a rolling basis. Each year a number of discretionary cost budgets are prepared from a zero base so that each one is reviewed, say, every three or four years. In the intervening years a form of the incremental approach is used for the budgets that are not subject to a ZBB exercise in that particular year.

11.5 Using budgets for control

We have already seen that the two activities of planning and control must go hand in hand. Carrying out the budgetary planning exercise without using the plan for control purposes is performing only part of the task. Budgetary planning and control activities are carried out in a continuous cycle as depicted in Figure 11.3.

Figure 11.3: The budgetary planning and control cycle

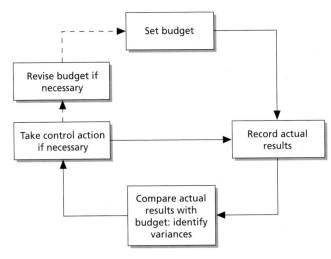

The differences revealed by the comparison of the actual results with the budget are called variances. An underspending is usually referred to as a favourable variance and an overspending an adverse variance.

An investigation of the variances may indicate that control action is required to attempt to bring the results back into line with budget. It may not be possible or desirable to correct all budget variances, particularly if circumstances have changed since the original budget was set. Nevertheless, managers should constantly monitor the level of budget variances, ensuring that they understand the reasons for them. This continuous monitoring will help to improve a manager's understanding of costs and their behaviour, so that the planning process can be continually refined each time it is repeated.

Towards the end of the budget period, many of the variances may be caused by the fact that the budget is no longer representative of current conditions. It may have been prepared perhaps fifteen months or more ago, so that now it is rather out of date.

Exercise

Can you identify any problems with using an out-of-date budget?

Solution

- It is not possible to tell which variances are in need of management action and which are the result of the out-of-date budget. Budgetary control is compromised.
- Managers may be demotivated if they feel they are being blamed for adverse variances over which they have no control.

These problems may be overcome by revising the budget part-way through the year, i.e. by updating the unexpired portion of the budget in the light of current circumstances, as shown in Figure 11.3.

This does not mean that the original budget will be discarded. It will still be necessary for managers to explain the total variance from the original budget. The difference is that part of the variance will be explained by the 'budget revision variance' so that management action can focus on the remaining variances, which are more likely to be controllable.

11.5.1 Budgetary control reports

There is no definitive layout for control reports, since they are prepared internally and may take any form that is useful to the organisation's managers. The reports will be designed to suit the purpose for which they are prepared, and certain data which is important in one context may not be important in another. However, it will be useful to review some examples so that you can get a feel for the way in which control reports might be prepared for different types of expenditure.

Figure 11.4: Extract from a revenue expenditure control report

Cost centre no: 435

Revenue expenditure – period 3   Date prepared:

Cost item	Expenditure this period		Expenditure to date			Comment
	Actual	Budget	Actual	Budget	Variance	
	£	£	£	£	£	
Salaries and payroll costs	10,690	9,970	32,160	29,970	(2,190)	One extra employee
Computer services	5,988	7,900	19,632	23,450	3,818	Major part of system still manual
Stationery	245	289	765	760	(5)	
Head office costs apportioned	1,290	1,000	3,788	2,900	(888)	Central overspending

Figure 11.5: Capital expenditure control report

North-east area factory: period 7
Improvement to staff canteen and rest area   Date prepared:
Capital expenditure authorisation code: 344

Expenditure this period	Expenditure to date	Forecast total cost on completion			Comment
		Actual	Budget	Variance	
£	£	£	£	£	
2,934	6,200	8,750	8,000	(750)	Overspend: auth. no: 348

The control report shown in Figure 11.4 enables management to exercise control by comparison. The report is designed to compare the actual expenditure with the budgeted expenditure to date and show the variance to date. Overspendings or adverse variances are shown in brackets.

Notice that variances are not shown for the expenditure in the period. This implies that in this particular case the cumulative figures are more important to management, therefore the period variance is omitted to avoid cluttering the report.

Management action may now be taken to correct any adverse circumstances or perhaps to maximise any favourable variances. Not all variances are controllable and a decision must be taken on which variances are worth further management investigation.

Exercise
Can you think of factors that you would consider before beginning an investigation into the cause of a variance?

Solution
You may have thought of the following factors:

- *The size of the variance.*
- *The likelihood of the variance being controllable when the cause is found.* For example, some types of variance, e.g. those caused by the price of a purchased material, may be caused by external factors which are outside managers' control.
- *The likely cost of the investigation.* Managers may know from past experience that the investigation of certain types of variance can be a lengthy and costly exercise which outweighs the benefit to be gained.
- *The likelihood of the variance being repeated in future periods.* Even a small variance can become significant on a cumulative basis if it arises repeatedly.

In the capital expenditure control report in Figure 11.5 no variances are shown for the expenditure to date or for the individual period. In this particular case management need to be aware of the eventual total cost of the project, and any expected overspending will then require separate authorisation.

Information concerning detailed variances is omitted from this particular report. This does not mean that such information is not available to managers. Following the exception principle this report has highlighted the most important variance. More detailed information on the expenditure and variances to date will probably be provided as subsidiary information.

11.5.2 Fixed and flexible budgets

When managers are comparing actual results with the budget for a period it is important to ensure that they are making a valid comparison. The use of flexible budgets can help to ensure that actual results are monitored against realistic targets. An example will demonstrate how flexible budgets may be used.

A company manufactures a single product and the following data shows results for the month of April, compared with the budgeted figures.

Operating statement for April (Adverse variances in brackets)

	Actual	Budget	Variance
Units produced and sold	1,000	1,200	(200)
	£	£	£
Sales revenue	110,000	120,000	(10,000)
Direct material	16,490	19,200	2,710
Direct labour	12,380	13,200	820
Overheads	61,920	61,400	(520)
Total costs	90,790	93,800	3,010
Profit	19,210	26,200	(6,990)

Looking at the costs incurred in April, a saving of £3,010 has been made, compared with budget. However, the number of units produced and sold was 200 less than budget, so some savings in expenditure might be expected. It is not possible to tell from this comparison how much of the saving is due to efficient cost control, and how much is the result of the reduction in activity.

Similarly, it is not possible to tell how much of the fall in sales revenue was due to the fall in activity. Some of the sales revenue variance may be the result of a difference in the sales price, but this budget comparison does not show the effect of this.

The type of budget in use here is a fixed budget. A fixed budget is one which remains unchanged regardless of the actual level of activity. In situations where activity levels are likely to change, and there is a significant proportion of variable costs, it is difficult to control expenditure satisfactorily with a fixed budget.

A flexible budget can help managers to make more valid comparisons. It is designed to show the expected revenue and the allowed expenditure for the actual number of units produced and sold. Comparing this flexible budget with the actual expenditure and revenue it is possible to distinguish genuine efficiencies.

11.5.3 Preparing a flexible budget

Before a flexible budget can be produced, managers must identify which costs are fixed and which are variable. The allowed expenditure on variable costs can then be increased or decreased as the level of activity changes. Fixed costs are those costs which will not increase or decrease over a given range of activity. The allowance for these items will therefore remain constant.

To continue with the example. Management have identified that the following budgeted costs are fixed:

	£
Direct labour	8,400
Overheads	53,000

It is now possible to identify the expected variable cost per unit produced and sold:

	Original budget (a)	Fixed cost (b)	Variable cost (c) = (a) – (b)	Variable cost/unit $^{(c)}/_{1,200}$
Units produced and sold	1,200			

	£	£	£	£
Direct material	19,200	–	19,200	16
Direct labour	13,200	8,400	4,800	4
Overheads	61,400	53,000	8,400	7
	93,800	61,400	32,400	27

Now that managers are aware of the fixed costs and the variable costs per unit it is possible to 'flex' the original budget to produce a budget cost allowance for 1,000 units produced and sold. The budget cost allowance for each item is calculated as follows:

Cost allowance = budgeted fixed cost + (number of units
produced and sold x variable cost per unit)

For the costs which are wholly fixed or wholly variable the calculation of the budget cost allowance is fairly straightforward. The remaining costs are semi-variable, which means that they are partly fixed and partly variable. For example, the budget cost allowance for direct labour is calculated as follows:

Cost allowance for direct labour = £8,400 + (1,000 x £4) = £12,400

The budgeted sales price per unit is $£120,000/1,200$ = £100 per unit. If it is assumed that sales revenues follow a linear variable pattern (i.e. the sales price remains constant) the full flexible budget can now be produced.

Exercise

Following the example of the calculation of the budget cost allowance for direct labour, calculate a revised budget cost allowance for all costs for an activity of 1,000 units and produce a revised variance statement for April.

Solution

Flexible budget comparison for April

	Flexible budget Cost/revenue allowances for 1,000 units			Actual	Variance
	Fixed	Variable	Total	cost/rev.	
	£	£	£	£	£
Sales revenue			100,000	110,000	10,000
Direct material	–	16,000	16,000	16,490	(490)
Direct labour	8,400	4,000	12,400	12,380	20
Overheads	53,000	7,000	60,000	61,920	(1,920)
	61,400	27,000	88,400	90,790	(2,390)
Profit			11,600	19,210	7,610

Note: variances in brackets are adverse.

This revised analysis shows that in fact the profit was £7,610 higher than would have been expected from a sales volume of 1,000 units.

The largest variance is a £10,000 favourable variance on sales revenue. This has arisen because a higher price was charged than budgeted. Could the higher sales price have been the cause of the shortfall in sales volume?

Although the answer to this question is not available from this information, without a flexed budget comparison it was not possible to tell that a different selling price had been charged.

 This is an example of variances which may be interrelated – i.e. a favourable variance on sales price may have caused an adverse variance on sales volume.

The cost variances in the flexible budget comparison are mainly adverse. These overspendings were not revealed when a fixed budget was used and managers may have been under the false impression that costs were being adequately controlled.

You may be wondering what has happened to the remainder of the £6,990 adverse profit variance shown in our original budget comparison at the beginning of this example. This could be analysed as follows:

Difference in budgeted profit caused by	
volume shortfall (£26,200 – £11,600)	(£14,600)
Profit variance from flexible budget comparison	£7,610
Total profit shortfall, per original budget comparison	(£6,990)

This shows clearly that the adverse variance was caused by the volume shortfall, and not by differences in the expected cost and revenues from the sales that were made.

11.5.4 Using flexible budgets for planning

Although flexible budgets can be useful for control purposes they are not particularly useful for planning. The original budget must contain a single target level of activity so that managers can plan such factors as the resource requirements and the product pricing policy. This would not be possible if they were faced with a range of possible activity levels.

11.6 Behavioural aspects of budgetary planning and control

A budgetary system does not consist only of accounting, forecasting and other management techniques. The success of a budgetary planning and control system depends on the cooperation of those who are to be involved in its operation. Individuals may not always behave in the best interests of the organisation, or they may be unwilling to strive to achieve the budget as set for the period. This is known as **dysfunctional behaviour**.

A budgetary system should be designed to minimise the occurrence of dysfunctional behaviour. This can be achieved if the system's designers and operators bear in mind the behavioural aspects of such systems. The human aspects to be considered are numerous and many of them are interrelated, but the following are the most important.

11.6.1 Motivation

A budgetary system will not be successful if individuals do not want to achieve the targets which have been set for their area of responsibility. A lack of the necessary motivation can exist for many reasons, including:

- The targets have not taken account of the individual's *aspiration level* – the level of performance which an individual has set as a personal target. If the performance target is set too far above the aspirational level, the individual will reject the budget as unrealistic and will be demotivated. If the target is set too far below the aspirational level the individual may also be demotivated by the lack of challenge, and may then work at a level of performance below that which could otherwise have been achieved. A department or section of an organisation can also have an aspiration level, which will be the collective result of all the individuals' aspiration levels.
- There is inadequate provision for the recognition of achievement. When performance levels have been achieved or exceeded it is important that managers acknowledge this and reward the relevant people. The reward need not necessarily be a financial one. A good manager will be able to motivate staff with appropriate 'psychological' reward – simply acknowledging the achievement may be sufficient.

11.6.2 Communication

Targets must be communicated in clear terms to those who are expected to achieve them. People cannot be expected to perform against a target they do not know about. It is also important that targets are understood – otherwise they will be rejected. Communication of actual results is also important: this is known as *feedback*.

11.6.3 Participation

Participative budgetary systems are usually the most successful. If the system is dictatorial, with imposed budgets, there is more likely to be dysfunctional behaviour. Individual managers should not simply be issued with their budgets without consultation. They should be consulted about their budgets during the planning process. Managers are then more likely to accept the targets contained in the budget when it is published.

A participative budgetary system will also encourage **goal congruence**. This exists when the budgetary system motivates individuals or groups to take actions that achieve their own personal goals while at the same time achieving those of the organisation. The system is designed so that there is a relationship between the company's goals and the individuals' goals. Goals are more likely to be congruent if individuals or groups have been involved in setting their own budgets.

Exercise
Can you think of a further, non-behavioural advantage of participative budgeting?

Solution
A further advantage of a participative process is that the quality of forecasting as a basis for the budget may improve. Managers who are in direct contact with the day-to-day activities of their part of the organisation will be more aware of current conditions and better able to predict any changes in the environment which may affect the budgetary forecast.

11.7 Summary

1. Budgets have two main roles: they act as authorities to spend or targets to achieve and as comparators for current performance.
2. Budgetary planning and control must go hand in hand. Carrying out the budgetary planning exercise without using the plan for control purposes is performing only part of the task.
3. A budget is set within the framework of an organisation's long-term plan. It is the first step towards the achievement of the long-term plan.
4. The need for co-ordination in the planning process is paramount.
5. The principal budget factor is the factor which limits the activities of the organisation.
6. The differences revealed by the comparison of the actual results with the budget are called variances.
7. Flexible budgets are designed to flex with changes in activity, to provide a realistic budget cost allowance for the actual level of activity achieved.
8. A successful budgetary planning and control system is designed with full consideration of the human aspects of budgeting.

Review questions

1. What are the two main roles of budgets? (section 11.2)
2. What is the role of the budget committee? (section 11.3.1)
3. Outline the contents of a budget manual. (section 11.3.2)
4. Why must the principal budget factor be identified at an early stage in the budgetary planning process? (section 11.3.3)
5. What is the difference between incremental and zero-based budgeting? (section 11.4)
6. Sketch the budgetary planning and control cycle (section 11.5)
7. What is a flexible budget? (section 11.5.2)
8. What is dysfunctional behaviour? (section 11.6)

Self-test questions

1. Comment critically on the following statements.
   (a) 'A budget is a forecast of an organisation's activities for the forth-coming period.'
   (b) 'The budgetary planning process for a manufacturing and trading organisation should always begin with the preparation of the sales budget.'
   (c) 'Revising the budget part way through the period is not advisable because it leads to a lack of continuity in the planning process.'

2. The fixed budget and actual results for G Ltd for the latest period are as follows.

	Budget	Actual
Production and sales	5,000 units	5,800 units
	£	£
Direct material	15,000	18,200
Direct labour	17,500	21,100
Variable overhead	10,000	11,000
Fixed overhead	14,000	15,000
Total cost	56,500	65,300
Sales revenue	80,000	93,400
Profit	23,500	28,100

Required

Prepare a flexible budget control report for the period, identifying the cost and revenue variances.

Answers to self-test questions

1. (a) A budget is not simply a forecast of forthcoming events. A forecast is a prediction of what might happen in future, given a particular set of circumstances. A budget is more than this. It is a planned result which an organisation is aiming to achieve. The budget may be based on the forecast, but the forecast acts only as a starting point in preparing the quantified budgetary plan.

(b) The budgetary planning process begins with the identification of the factor that limits the organisation's activities, the principal budget factor. Often this is the sales volume, but for a manufacturing organisation it could be a factor of production such as machine capacity or labour hours. The budget for the principal budget factor should be prepared first, then all other budgets are co-ordinated to this.

(c) A budget is usually prepared a few weeks or months before the start of the budget period, so that by the end of the period the original budgetary plan might be as much as a year old. Therefore it is unlikely to represent a useful tool for short-term planning and control. In this situation it is common to revise the unexpired portion of the budget so that it represents a realistic yardstick for planning and control purposes.

This does not mean that the original budget is discarded. Instead, a budget revision variance is often used to highlight the difference between the original and revised budgets. Managers can use this to guide their forecasting and planning activities in future budgeting exercises, so that the budgetary planning process is continually refined.

2. The flexible budget for 5,800 units will include extra cost allowances for all the variable costs, but not for the fixed overhead.

Production and sales	Original budget 5,000 units	Flexible budget 5,800 units	Actual results 5,800 units	Variance
	£	£	£	£
Direct material	15,000 $(x\,5,800/5,000)$	17,400	18,200	(800)
Direct labour	17,500	20,300	21,100	(800)
Variable overhead	10,000	11,600	11,000	600
Fixed overhead	14,000	14,000	15,000	(1,000)
Total cost	56,500	63,300	65,300	(2,000)
Sales revenue	80,000 $(x\,5,800/5,000)$	92,800	93,400	600
Profit	23,500	29,500	28,100	(1,400)

Note: variances in brackets are adverse.

Glossary

Introduction

This glossary contains the main financial terms that might be encountered by the non-specialist. The definitions and descriptions are taken from *Management Accounting: Official Terminology* published by the Chartered Institute of Management Accountants (CIMA), which contains a more extensive terminology. The glossary is divided into logical groupings which follow the structure of CIMA's *Terminology*.

Accounting concepts and terms

Accounting
- The classification and recording of monetary transactions; and
- The presentation and interpretation of the results of those transactions in order to assess performance over a period and the financial position at a given date; and
- The monetary projection of future activities arising from alternative planned courses of action.

Accounting standard
Authoritative statement of how particular types of transaction and other events should be reflected in financial statements. Compliance with accounting standards will normally be necessary for financial statements to give a true and fair view (ASB).

Accounting Standards Board (ASB)
A UK standard-setting body established on 1 August 1990 to develop, issue and withdraw accounting standards. Its aims are 'to establish and improve standards of financial accounting and reporting, for the benefit of users, preparers and auditors of financial information' (ASB).

Financial accounting

The classification and recording of the monetary transactions of an entity in accordance with established concepts, principles, accounting standards and legal requirements and their presentation, by means of profit and loss accounts, balance sheets and cash-flow statements, during and at the end of an accounting period.

Management accounting

The application of the principles of accounting and financial management to create, protect, preserve and increase value so as to deliver that value to the stakeholders of profit and not-for-profit enterprises, both public and private. Management accounting is an integral part of management, requiring the identification, generation, presentation, interpretation and use of information relevant to:

- formulating business strategy;
- planning and controlling activities;
- decision-making;
- efficient resource usage;
- performance improvement and value enhancement;
- safeguarding tangible and intangible assets;
- corporate governance and internal control.

Net realisable value

The amount for which an asset could be disposed, less any direct selling costs (FRS10).

Cost ascertainment and cost management

Absorbed overhead

Overhead attached to products or services by means of absorption rates.
Under- or *over-absorbed overhead*
The difference between overhead incurred and overhead absorbed, using an estimated rate, in a given period.

Activity-based costing (ABC)

An approach to the costing and monitoring of activities which involves tracing resource consumption and costing final outputs. Resources are assigned to activities and activities to cost objects based on consumption estimates. The latter utilise cost drivers to attach activity costs to outputs.

Avoidable costs

The specific costs of an activity or sector of a business which would be avoided if that activity or sector did not exist.

Contribution

Sales value less variable cost of sales. It may be expressed as total contribution, contribution per unit or as a percentage of sales.

Cost behaviour

The variability of input costs with activity undertaken. A number of cost behaviour patterns are possible, ranging from variable costs whose cost level varies directly with the level of activity, to fixed costs, where changes in output have no effect upon the cost level.

Cost driver

Any factor which causes a change in the cost of an activity, e.g. the quality of parts received by an activity is a determining factor in the work required by that activity and therefore affects the resources required. An activity may have multiple cost drivers associated with it.

Differential/incremental cost

The difference in total cost between alternatives; calculated to assist decision-making.

Direct cost

Expenditure which can be economically identified with and specifically measured in respect to a relevant cost object.

Discretionary cost

A cost whose amount within a time period is determined by, and is easily altered by, a decision taken by the appropriate budget holder. Marketing, research and training are generally regarded as discretionary costs. Control of discretionary costs is through the budgeting process. Also known as managed or policy costs.

First in, first out (FIFO)

The principle that the oldest items or costs are the first to be used. Most commonly applied to the pricing of issues of materials, based on using first the costs of the oldest materials in stock, *irrespective of the sequence in which actual material usage takes place*. Closing stock is therefore generally valued at relatively current costs.

Fixed cost
A cost which is incurred for an accounting period, and which, within certain output or turnover limits, tends to be unaffected by fluctuations in the level of activity (output or turnover).

Marginal cost
The part of the cost of one unit of product or service which would be avoided if that unit were not produced, or which would increase if one extra unit were produced.

Operational gearing
The relationship of the fixed cost to the total cost of an operating unit. The greater the proportion of total costs that are fixed (high operational gearing), the greater is the advantage to the organisation of increasing sales volume. Conversely, should sales volume drop, a highly geared organisation would find the high proportion of fixed costs to be a major problem, possibly causing a rapid swing from profitability into significant loss-making.

Opportunity cost
The value of the benefit sacrificed when one course of action is chosen in preference to an alternative. The opportunity cost is represented by the forgone potential benefit from the best rejected course of action.

Overhead absorption rate
A means of attributing overhead to a product or service, based for example on direct labour hours, direct labour cost or machine hours.

Overhead/indirect cost
Expenditure on labour, materials or services which cannot be economically identified with a specific saleable cost unit. The synonymous term 'burden' is in common use in the USA and in subsidiaries of American companies in the UK.

Prime cost
The total cost of direct material, direct labour and direct expenses.

Product cost
The cost of a finished product built up from its cost elements.

Production cost
Prime cost plus absorbed production overhead.

Relevant costs/revenues

Costs and revenues appropriate to a specific management decision.

Semi-variable cost/semi-fixed cost/mixed cost

A cost containing both fixed and variable components and which is thus partly affected by a change in the level of activity.

Sunk costs

Costs that have been irreversibly incurred or committed prior to a decision point and which cannot therefore be considered relevant to subsequent decisions. Sunk costs may also be termed *irrecoverable costs*.

Variable cost

A cost which varies with a measure of activity.

Planning

Breakeven chart

A chart which indicates approximate profit or loss at different levels of sales volume within a limited range.

Breakeven point

The level of activity at which there is neither profit nor loss. It can be ascertained by using a breakeven chart or by calculation.

Cost–volume–profit (CVP) analysis

The study of the effects on future profit of changes in fixed cost, variable cost, sales price, quantity and mix.

Goal congruence

In a control system, the state which leads individuals or groups to take actions which are in their self-interest and also in the best interest of the entity.

Strategic plan

A statement of long-term goals along with a definition of the strategies and policies which will ensure achievement of these goals.

Budgeting

Budget

A quantitative statement, for a defined period of time, which may include planned revenues, expenses, assets, liabilities and cash flows. A budget provides a focus for the organisation, aids the coordination of activities, and facilitates control. Planning is achieved by means of a fixed master budget, whereas control is generally exercised through the comparison of actual costs with a flexible budget.

Budget centre

A section of an entity for which control may be exercised and budgets prepared.

Budget cost allowance/flexed budget

The budgeted cost ascribed to the level of activity achieved in a budget centre in a control period. It comprises variable costs in direct proportion to volume achieved and fixed costs as a proportion of the annual budget.

Budget period

The period for which a budget is prepared and used, which may then be subdivided into control periods.

Budget slack

The intentional overestimation of expenses and/or underestimation of revenues in the budgeting process.

Budgetary control

The establishment of budgets relating the responsibilities of executives to the requirements of a policy, and the continuous comparison of actual with budgeted results, either to secure by individual action the objectives of that policy or to provide a basis for its revision.

Fixed budget

A budget which is normally set prior to the start of an accounting period, and which is not changed in response to subsequent changes in activity or costs/revenues. Fixed budgets are generally used for planning purposes.

Flexible budget

A budget which, by recognising different cost behaviour patterns, is designed to change as volume of activity changes.

Imposed/top-down budget
A budget allowance which is set without permitting the ultimate budget holder to have the opportunity to participate in the budgeting process.

Incremental budgeting
A method of budget setting in which the prior period budget is used as a base for the current budget, which is set by adjusting the prior period budget to take account of any anticipated changes.

Management by exception
The practice of focusing on activities which require attention and ignoring those which appear to be conforming to expectation.

Master budget
The budget into which all subsidiary budgets are consolidated, normally comprising budgeted profit and loss account, budgeted balance sheet and budgeted cash-flow statement. These documents, and the supporting subsidiary budgets, are used to plan and control activities for the following year.

Participative/bottom-up budgeting
A budgeting system in which all budget holders are given the opportunity to participate in setting their own budgets.

Principal budget factor
A factor which will limit the activities of an undertaking and which is often the starting point in budget preparation.

Relevant range
The activity levels within which assumptions about cost behaviour in breakeven analysis remain valid.

Zero-based budgeting
A method of budgeting which requires each cost element to be specifically justified, as though the activities to which the budget relates were being undertaken for the first time. Without approval, the budget allowance is zero.

Financial accounts

Accrued expenses

Charges which are brought into the financial statements at the end of a period because, although goods and services have been provided, they have not yet been charged for by the suppliers. For example, electricity, invoiced in arrears, generally requires accrual at the end of each accounting period.

Assets

Rights or other access to future economic benefits controlled by an entity as a result of past transactions or events (FRS 5).

Intangible assets

Non-financial fixed assets that do not have physical substance but are identifiable and are controlled by the entity through custody or legal rights (FRS 10)

Tangible assets

Assets which have a physical identity, e.g. plant and machinery.

Capital employed

The funds used by an entity for its operations. This can be expressed in various ways depending upon the purpose of the computation. For example, for operations evaluation capital employed may be defined as the total value of non-current assets plus working capital, whereas for investor evaluation owners' capital plus reserves may be used.

Capital expenditure

The cost of acquiring, producing or enhancing fixed assets. See revenue expenditure.

Corporation tax

Tax chargeable on companies resident in the UK or trading in the UK through a branch or agency, as well as on certain unincorporated associations.

Cost of sales

The sum of variable cost of sales plus factory overhead attributable to the sales. In management accounts this may be referred to as production cost of sales or cost of goods sold.

Creditor

A person or an entity to whom money is owed as a consequence of the receipt of goods or services in advance of payment.

Current asset

Cash or other assets, e.g. stock, debtors and short-term investments, held for conversion into cash in the normal course of trading.

Current liabilities

Liabilities which fall due for payment within one year. They include that part of long-term loans due for repayment within one year.

Debtor

A person or an entity owing money.

Depreciation

The measure of the cost or revalued amount of the economic benefits of the tangible fixed asset that have been consumed during the period.

Consumption includes wearing out, using up or other reduction in the useful economic life of a tangible fixed asset whether arising from use, effluxion of time or obsolescence through either changes in technology or demand for the goods and services produced by the asset (FRS 15).

Dividend

An amount payable to shareholders from profits or other distributable reserves. Dividends are normally paid in cash, but scrip dividends, paid by the issue of additional shares, are permissible. Listed companies normally pay two dividends per year, an interim dividend, based on interim profits reported during the accounting period, and a final dividend, based on the final audited accounts and approved at the Annual General Meeting.

Equity

The issued ordinary share capital plus reserves, statutory and otherwise, which represent the investment in a company by the ordinary shareholders.

Fixed asset

Any asset, tangible or intangible, acquired for retention by an entity for the purpose of providing a service to the business, and not held for resale in the normal course of trading.

Goodwill (purchased goodwill)

The difference between the cost of an acquired entity and the aggregate of the fair value of that entity's identifiable assets and liabilities.

Liquid assets

Cash, and other assets readily convertible into cash – e.g. short-term investments.

Net assets/net worth
The excess of book value of assets over liabilities, including loan capital. This is equivalent to net worth, which is used to describe the paid-up share capital and reserves.

Net book value/written-down value
The historical cost of an asset less any accumulated depreciation or other provision for diminution in value, e.g. a reduction to net realisable value, or asset value which has been revalued downwards to reflect market conditions.

Prepayments
Expenditure on goods or services for future benefit which is to be charged to future operations, e.g. rentals paid in advance. These amounts are included in current assets.

Reserves
Retained profits or surpluses. In a not-for-profit entity these are described as accumulated funds. Reserves may be distributable (revenue reserves) or non-distributable (capital reserves).

Revenue expenditure
Expenditure on the manufacture of goods, the provision of services or on the general conduct of the entity, which is charged to the profit and loss account in the accounting period of sale. This includes repairs and depreciation of fixed assets, as distinct from the provision of these assets. See capital expenditure.

Working capital
The capital available for conducting the day-to-day operations of an organisation; normally the excess of current assets over current liabilities.

Index